A Short Guide to Writing About Criminal Justice

A Short Guide to Writing About Criminal Justice

Charles Piltch

John Jay College of Criminal Justice,
City University of New York (CUNY)

Karen J. Terry

John Jay College of Criminal Justice,
City University of New York (CUNY)

Prentice Hall

Boston   Columbus   Indianapolis   New York   San Francisco   Upper Saddle River   Amsterdam
Cape Town   Dubai   London   Madrid   Milan   Munich   Paris   Montreal   Toronto   Delhi
Mexico City   Sao Paulo   Sydney   Hong Kong   Seoul   Singapore   Taipei   Tokyo

Vice President and Executive Publisher: Vernon Anthony
Senior Acquisitions Editor: Eric Krassow
Editorial Assistant: Lynda Cramer
Media Project Manager: Karen Bretz
Director of Marketing: David Gesell
Marketing Manager: Adam Kloza
Senior Marketing Coordinator: Alicia Wozniak
Production Manager: Renata Butera
Creative Director: Jayne Conte
Cover Design: Suzanne Behnke
Full-Service Project Management/Composition: Rakesh Poddar/Aptara®, Inc.
Printer/Binder: Strategic Content Imaging

Library of Congress Cataloging-in-Publication Data
Piltch, Charles.
    A short guide to writing about criminal justice / Charles Piltch, Karen J. Terry.
        p. cm.
    Includes bibliographical references and index.
    ISBN-13: 978-0-13-802902-9
    ISBN-10: 0-13-802902-4
    1. Criminology—Authorship.   2. Criminal justice, Administration of—Authorship.
3. Academic writing—Handbooks, manuals, etc.   I. Terry, Karen J.   II. Title.
    HV6024.5.P55 2011
    808'.06364—dc22

                                                            2010012027

10 9 8 7 6 5 4 3 2 1
Prentice Hall
is an imprint of

www.pearsonhighered.com   ISBN-13: 978-0-13-802902-9
                           ISBN-10:   0-13-802902-4

BRIEF CONTENTS

CONTENTS

PREFACE

Writing in the field of criminal justice can be challenging for students of all levels, and the purpose of this book is to help students navigate that writing process. Criminal justice courses are based upon theoretical, practical, experiential, and policy-based issues, and students must understand how to think and write about issues from multiple perspectives.

Criminal justice is unique in that nearly everyone has some knowledge of the field, most often from television (*CSI, Law and Order*), movies (*Silence of the Lambs*), news sources (newspapers and TV news shows), and personal experience (traffic tickets, being the victim of a crime). However, students in criminal justice must take this tacit knowledge of the subject further when studying, and learn how to think objectively about critical issues. It is not enough to *feel* like the death penalty is wrong, for instance; it is necessary to read empirical research about capital punishment; think critically about the pros and cons of this policy; and make arguments about whether, for who, and in what circumstances it should be a form of punishment in the United States. Importantly, the way students will convey this knowledge is usually through writing.

Academic writing does not come naturally, especially that which must be objectively presented for fields like criminal justice. Every academic course that students take leads to a new process of learning what to do and how to do it. This book discusses the major approaches to writing in criminal justice and outlines for students how to think and write from various perspectives. Criminal justice is an interdisciplinary field and students must understand how to write from a legal, theoretical, and policy-based perspective. This requires different types of research, different ways of approaching issues, and different writing styles. This book presents information about writing assignments in classes, as well as writing research assignments from these different perspectives. The book is structured so that it contains general information about writing in the beginning, but with specific guidelines on how this can be applied to criminal justice writing. The second part of the book contains sample writing assignments for various courses in criminal justice. It provides students with a guide about how to think and write about the questions while applying the information from the first part. The third part of the book focuses on research in criminal justice, and how students should find, write about, and present their research. The goal is to have students understand general writing guidelines and apply these to their course and research assignments to improve their writing approaches and techniques in all areas of criminal justice.

ACKNOWLEDGMENTS

We would like to thank Kelly Villella at Longman, who approached us with the idea for this book and helped us out along the way, and Ginny Blanford, who has worked with us since. We would also like to thank the reviewers of our text who helped us to shape its development and provided us with valuable assistance. These include: David Baker, The University of Toledo; Deborah Baskin, California State University–Los Angeles; Bruce L. Berg, California State University–Long Beach; Alton Braddock, University of Louisiana–Monroe; Tod W. Burke, Radford University; Maryann Cama, Youngstown State University; Dennis W. Catlin, Northern Arizona University–Tuscon; Jan Hagemann, San Jose State University; Craig Hemmens, Boise State University; Christine Ludowise, Georgia Southern University; Jean M. McGloin, University of Maryland; Joan Mullin, University of Texas; Barbara Perry, University of Ontario Institute of Technology; Larry Snyder, Herkimer County Community College; Elizabeth Quinn, Fayetteville State University; Christine E. Rasche, University of North Florida; Michael S. Vaughn, Georgia State University; Renee F. Williams, Chicago State University; and Bodhan Yaworsky, New Jersey City University.

This effort could never have been successful without the assistance of our colleagues at John Jay College of Criminal Justice, who offered us support, insight, and ideas. As Charles notes, one could not be a member of an English Department in a Liberal Arts College of Criminal Justice without spending much time thinking, writing, and conversing about the relationship of writing and criminal justice. He has also benefited from dialogue with other CUNY colleagues working in testing and "Writing Across the Curriculum," and especially from those colleagues, students, and Writing Fellows who joined him in "Writing Across the Curriculum" at John Jay. He owes debts too numerous to mention to the giants in rhetoric and composition, especially Flower and Hayes, Fahnestock and Secor, Barbara Walvoord, and his friend Chuck Bazerman. Karen would like to thank those in the Criminal Justice department at John Jay College as well as her research assistant, Odessa Simms, for her assistance with ideas for the book.

No major effort can be undertaken without the support of family and friends. Charles would like to thank his wife Ziva, who has given him a lifetime of every kind of support (intellectual, spiritual, and practical), and Karen would like to thank her husband, Stephen, who has always supported her throughout her career.

A Short Guide to Writing About Criminal Justice

Overview of Criminal Justice Writing

1
INTRODUCTION TO WRITING IN CRIMINAL JUSTICE

The aim of this book is to teach students how to write in the interdisciplinary field of criminal justice. It will teach students how to think about criminal justice questions, approach these questions, and write about topical issues in the field. It will be useful for students taking courses in the field of criminal justice, broadly defined, as well as those writing research papers in this field. Colleges offer criminal justice courses at the associate, bachelor's, master's, and doctorate levels. Though this book is primarily geared toward undergraduate students, it can also be helpful to graduate students who are writing research papers.

Criminal justice is a large and varied field of study, influenced by disciplines such as psychology, sociology, anthropology, history, science, and law. It is both theoretical and practical, and includes the study of why individuals commit crime and how to implement policies that will be effective at preventing deviant behavior. Students who study criminal justice will need to understand the criminal justice system (policing, courts, and corrections), as well as how to read and write about issues in the humanities, social sciences, and the law. Despite this broad context, it is important still for students to understand the basics of writing in any field and to apply writing standards to criminal justice topics.

Many writing books take a simplistic view of "writing." Writing is not just style or putting thinking into the appropriate words. Writing is a basic tool of thinking, not merely its end product. Reading, thinking, and writing are interdependent. The process of writing something for a course involves different kinds of reading, thinking, and writing at all stages of the assignment, and this book explains how these processes are linked. As students gain more familiarity with topics in the field of criminal justice, they can expand their repertoire of skills and experience of conceiving, planning, researching, reflecting, drafting, evaluating, and revising through writing.

Most students have had courses, such as English Composition, where it did not matter so much *what* was said as *how* it was said. Writing for criminal justice is not like that. The chief purpose of the writing is to communicate content to the reader, and the writing is likely to be judged mostly or entirely on its content. In criminal justice courses, writing is a record of the students' thinking, expressed in a visible and permanent form. This book thus puts most of its effort into helping the reader understand the sorts of assignments likely to be given, helping to figure out what should be accomplished in the assignment or research project, how to think through it, and how to make sure that the final product is the best possible expression of the thought.

This is not to say that what students learn in core writing courses is not relevant in the field of criminal justice. This book simply puts what has already been learned into a different perspective. In most colleges, students do not begin the study of criminal justice prior to completing, or at least beginning, core writing courses. Among other purposes, these introductory writing courses are supposed to prepare students for later academic writing in content courses, and teachers of those content courses assume that students have mastered basic writing. That means students know about the basic rhetoric of introduction, body, and conclusion, and something about the construction of the sentence and paragraph. It often means that students have familiarity and some practice with basic rhetorical modes like narration, description, comparison, and causal analysis, albeit not specifically in a content-specific or disciplinary context such as criminal justice. For many criminal justice professors, it especially means that students have sufficient mastery of basic writing, grammar, spelling, style, and usage. In many colleges, these core courses are supplemented with a physical or Online Writing Lab (OWL) to help students continue to develop basic writing competencies, but upon completion of the basic courses, the responsibility of writing correctly is generally on the student. If teachers in content courses, like criminal justice, discuss writing in the classroom or hand out material about how to write, it is almost always in regard to expectations specific to the course or the discipline.

STRUCTURE OF THE BOOK

This book is about students taking responsibility for themselves as criminal justice writers and understanding the various perspectives of this field. It provides the tools that students will need to excel in this capacity. The first section, "Overview of Criminal Justice Writing," addresses the core competencies needed to write in the field of criminal justice. This section is more general than the two that follow, in that it is meant to be useful to all criminal justice courses. This first chapter provides an overview of the book, including the considerations of writing in the field of criminal justice. Chapter 2 is an explanation of the "rhetorical situation," or the need for the student to determine the purpose of an assignment, the audience for the assignment, and the persona that should be projected in the writing. Although assignments in all classes require an understanding of the rhetorical situation, this book focuses on the unique rhetorical situation that should be considered in different types of criminal justice classes. Chapter 3 provides an overview of how students learn to tailor the writing process to each assignment. It includes a discussion of each step of the writing process, from reading and note-taking to editing the final draft of a writing assignment. Chapter 4 contains a description of the four types of general writing skills most in demand in criminal justice writing—summary, critical analysis, comparison, and causal analysis—all learned in the context of actual Criminal Justice assignments.

The next section, "Writing for Criminal Justice Courses," distinguishes the kinds of writing done in different areas of criminal justice study. Because criminal justice is such a vast field, it is important to understand how to write in multiple contexts. This section contains three chapters. Chapter 5 focuses on criminal justice, policing, courts, and corrections courses. These require the student to have an understanding of the agencies in the criminal justice system, and writing assignments in these classes often focus on policy-oriented writing. Chapter 6 is an overview of writing in criminology and victimology courses. Unlike the policy-based courses on the criminal justice system, writing assignments in these courses are often theoretically focused and require explanations of why individuals commit offenses or are victimized. Finally, Chapter 7 focuses on writing assignments in legal studies courses. These vary substantially from the criminal justice and criminology courses and require unique writing assignments, such as case briefs, that have a specific format. All of these types of courses require students to understand the information about writing generally, as explained in the first section of the book.

The final section of the book, "Research-Oriented Writing," will help students with basic research, writing, and presentation skills. The focus of Chapter 8 is the literature review. It provides an overview of what a literature review is, the type of information that it should contain, and how to find and summarize information from different types of sources for it. Chapter 9 is a summary of the styles of referencing, with a focus on types of citation styles and the most common ones used in the field of criminal justice. The primary focus is on APA (American Psychological Association) style referencing, which is the most common in the field, though it also provides a brief explanation of the ASA (American Sociological Association) and MLA (Modern Language Association) referencing systems. The final chapter of the book focuses on presentations and visual aids such as charts, tables, and figures that can be used in both research writing and oral presentations. This information can also be useful for students taking criminal justice classes who need to give oral presentations as part of their course.

CRIMINAL JUSTICE AS A UNIQUE DISCIPLINE

A Short Guide to Writing About Criminal Justice is one in a series of student guides for writing in a particular academic discipline. This topic differs from the others in two important ways. First, criminal justice is a multidisciplinary field in the way that few others are, and second, it has a real-world connection that is unique in academia. As such, professors in different types of courses will have varying expectations for the style of writing, content of the assignments, and applications of key issues. This book outlines what those expectations are and what to expect in different types of classes. It also outlines the benefits and problems with bringing to the study of criminal justice prior knowledge about the topic.

A Multidisciplinary View of Criminal Justice

The study of criminal justice is necessarily multidisciplinary. Though disciplines such as history tend to be studied from a single perspective, criminal justice is multidisciplinary and studied from a variety of perspectives. This book recognizes what the various disciplines share and what is unique to each. It is helpful at the outset to recognize the different kinds of courses and different kinds of writing that make up the field of criminal justice.

Some criminal justice courses are concerned with the social sciences and focus on the activities within and people involved in the criminal justice system, including offenders, victims, police, judges, juries, lawyers, and corrections officers. These courses are most often taught by professors with training in sociology, psychology, criminology, and anthropology, and they primarily involve developing, understanding, testing, and applying theories of behavior for the above-mentioned groups.

Other criminal justice courses have more direct practical goals and are concerned with the agencies that constitute the criminal justice system (the police, courts, and correctional services). These courses may be taught by professors with field experience in particular agencies or with backgrounds in government and public administration. Theoretical and legal issues are important, but in these classes the emphasis is on defining and solving current or potential problems with the system, understanding criminal justice policies, and analyzing their effectiveness.

Still other criminal justice courses are entirely or partly concerned with the law, especially constitutional law and its impact on the criminal justice system. These courses are usually taught by lawyers or professors with a law degree. Writing in these courses involves summarizing, comparing, and applying laws and especially actual or hypothetical case studies. It often requires and embodies legal research.

Because of the multidisciplinary nature of criminal justice, students in this field can graduate with a wealth of knowledge and experiences that are unique in academia. It is excellent for the student's intellectual growth to be exposed to the diversity of topics, methods, and purposes in the various disciplines and subdisciplines. It is an enriching academic experience to approach a topic such as juvenile delinquency from the legal perspective (e.g., how the law expects different behavior from juveniles than from adults, how different correctional or rehabilitative strategies are open to juveniles), from the sociological perspective (e.g., how schooling helps or hinders the growth of gangs), from the psychological perspective (e.g., what needs delinquent behavior serves), and from the institutional perspective (e.g., how juvenile justice courts should function). Different perspectives, different bodies of knowledge, and different methodologies ought to enrich the student's understanding of the subject. However, all this diversity also increases the need for students to understand the perspective from which to study, analyze, and write about particular topics. What is appropriate for one class may differ substantially from others, even when the classes are covering the same topic.

Linking Scholarship to the Real World

Most people will read, see, or hear about something related to the criminal justice process daily, either through personal experience or through various media outlets. Because of this, criminal justice students begin their studies with more experience and knowledge than they typically bring to a more traditional academic discipline. This prior access to information about criminal justice gives students more of a sense of what criminal justice is—including its agencies, practitioners, and issues—than is true for most disciplines.

To begin thinking about what you already know about criminal justice, see Box 1.1. Think about where you have gained knowledge about criminal justice, through personal experience, news reports, or movies, and how accurate that knowledge is likely to be. The study of criminal justice will provide you with more formal information about the criminal justice system, including information from federal and state agencies and studies published by academics about those agencies.

Because criminal justice topics are regularly in the news, in movies, and on television, it is easy to develop beliefs about this field that are more fiction than fact. Although television dramas are beneficial, in that they bring to the forefront topics of great importance (e.g., *Law & Order: SVU* looks at the issues related to sexual assault and abuse), they also convey some false images (e.g., in *CSI: Miami* physical evidence is analyzed immediately and crimes are solved expeditiously). The academic study of criminal justice will dispel these myths, but at the outset it is important to understand some key facts about criminal justice. See Box 1.2 for some common myths about crime and criminal justice that may result from television, movies, and news.

Also unique to this field are the real-world applications of academic knowledge and the importance of knowledge in this field. For example, domestic violence is a serious problem in the United States and elsewhere, but what are the appropriate responses to this problem? What should the police do when facing the respond to a call for domestic violence? How should this be handled in the courts? Do informal or formal criminal justice responses work better at reducing future incidents of

BOX 1.1
What Do You Know About Crime and Criminal Justice?

People are exposed to criminal justice issues on a daily basis, either through personal experience, reports in the news, or entertainment channels. How much do you know about crime and justice? Look at the following questions to begin thinking about these issues.

WHAT DO YOU KNOW ABOUT CRIME?

- Have you ever been the victim of a crime?
- Do you know anyone who has been the victim of a crime?
- Have you ever heard reports about the "crime rate"? Do you know what this means?
- Are you afraid of becoming the victim of a crime?
- Do you take any precautions against being the victim of a crime? If so, what are they (e.g., lock the doors at night, avoid walking alone at night) and why?
- Do local politicians address crime issues in their campaigns or press releases? What sorts of things do they say?
- Do you watch movies or television series about crime and detection? How realistic are these shows?

WHAT DO YOU KNOW ABOUT POLICING?

- Have you ever met a police officer?
- Have you ever reported a crime to the police?
- Have you ever gotten a ticket (e.g., speeding, parking, jaywalking)?
- Have you ever been stopped, questioned, or frisked by the police?
- Have you ever been arrested or spent time in a station house or jail?
- What is your opinion of the police based upon:
  - Television shows (e.g., *The Shield, Law and Order, The Wire*)

- News reports (e.g., arresting criminals, conducting investigations, committing acts of corruption or misconduct)
- Friends/family members who have interacted with the police
- Interactions such as with D.A.R.E. or G.R.E.A.T. programs in schools
- Seeing them in the community (e.g., on foot patrol, at parades or other events, on a subway)

WHAT DO YOU KNOW ABOUT COURTS?

- Have you ever been in a courtroom? If so, what type (e.g., criminal court, family court, civil court)?
- Have you ever served on a jury? If so:
  - Did it go to deliberation?
  - Were the judge's instructions helpful?
  - Did you feel comfortable with your decision?
  - How did you feel about the jury process?
- Do you know what the roles are of the prosecutor and the defense attorney?
- What do you know about the legal system from watching the news or reading the newspaper?

WHAT DO YOU KNOW ABOUT CORRECTIONS?

- Have you ever been incarcerated or served a criminal sentence in the community (e.g., probation)?
- Have you ever been inside a prison?
- Have you ever seen people serving a community sentence (e.g., picking up trash on the side of a road)?
- Do you know what the restrictions are on felons (e.g., can't own firearms, can't vote in many jurisdictions)?
- Do you think offenders can be reformed?
- What do movies like *Shawshank Redemption* tell us about prisoner reentry?

BOX 1.2
The Myths of the Criminal Justice System

Many of the most popular shows on television relate to crime or criminal justice agencies. Movies, too, often center around criminals and their behaviors. These media portrayals of criminals are usually exaggerated, they focus on extreme cases of psychologically motivated offenders, and they are usually apprehended in time for the final commercial. Sadly, these are not average offenders and the criminal justice system is rarely such a cohesive, well-functioning network of agencies. Here are some examples of common misperceptions or myths based upon popular television shows and movies:

- Crime cases are solved in an hour. Unlike the cases that are portrayed in most crime dramas on television: (a) not all crimes are solved, (b) those that are often take a long time to be solved, and (c) solving these cases rarely relies on testing physical evidence (e.g., DNA).
- Offenders are strangers. To increase the drama in television and movies, criminals are often portrayed as strangers to their victims. In fact, most perpetrators know their victims.
- The police are always involved in law-enforcement activity. Television shows often show car chases, the hot pursuit of criminals, and officers with guns drawn. However, police officers spend most of their time conducting order-maintenance activities, and only about 10 percent of their time is actually filled with typical law-enforcement duties.
- A degree in Criminal Justice will lead to a job as a crime scene investigator. Some television shows blur the lines of science and social science. Criminalistics is the study of physical evidence from a crime and is a science-based study. Those who study criminalistics are employed at crime labs and study such things as ballistics, fibers, and other types of physical evidence. This specialization is not to be confused with criminologists, who study why individuals commit crimes and empirically test theories about the causes of criminal behavior.
- Profiling serial killers is a common activity in the field of criminal justice. Thanks to movies like *The Silence of the Lambs* and television shows like *Criminal Minds*, many criminal justice students mistakenly believe that they will get a job profiling criminals, particularly high-profile offenders like Hannibal Lecter. The study of criminal justice is much more practical, however, and focuses on issues such as crime prevention policies (e.g., whether the presence of closed-circuit television monitors deters criminal behavior, and whether mandatory arrest policies reduce recidivism in domestic violence offenders).
- Crime is increasing. With the proliferation of 24-hour news channels, many news programs focus on exciting, but negative, news stories that are often centered around crimes. This increased focus on criminal behavior may lead people to believe that crime is increasing, but in fact, crime has been decreasing, or has at least reached a plateau, in most jurisdictions in the United States.

violence? The study of criminal justice will lend information and advance knowledge to this topic that can be applied in the real world and reduce serious cases of offending behavior.

This book means to help students be aware both of the rewards and the risks of the multi-disciplinary richness that is the study of criminal justice. The book allows students to develop a repertoire of approaches to criminal justice writing that should stand them in good stead wherever they find themselves.

Summary

Criminal justice is a multidisciplinary field, and the study of criminal justice has important real-world implications. By understanding issues related to crime and justice from numerous perspectives, it is possible to better understand why crime happens, how agencies work to deal with perpetrators and victims, and what types of policies are put in place to control and prevent crime. Writing in criminal justice classes poses a unique challenge because of the multidisciplinary nature of the field. Students must understand the perspective from which they are studying a topic so as to know how to think about, research, analyze, and respond to the issues. This book will help students to do that.

2 | THE RHETORICAL SITUATION OF THE CRIMINAL JUSTICE STUDENT WRITER

Writing about criminal justice is like anything else you do: the more you know about the task and the better prepared you are for it, the easier it is and the better the outcome. Writing is a form of communication, and it may help to compare it to another, more familiar kind of communication: speaking. People usually do not consciously prepare for what they are going to say in a conversation or how they are going to say it, because talking is such a natural activity. People do not rehearse conversations or practice language before speaking, particularly for casual conversations. It is only when the person being spoken to does not understand what is being said or is getting a negative impression of the speaker that the conversant may hesitate or reconsider what has been said. Generally, speaking to friends allows for an informal atmosphere where each person can act and speak informally, correcting their language by responding to personal cues when necessary. Conversations with friends do not revolve around making first impressions, which were made long ago, or judgments, as the friendship has already been established.

Talking to strangers or giving a formal talk, on the other hand, requires more thought. It is necessary to consider what you will say and how you are going to say it. The more the talking counts, the more self-conscious a person becomes and the more that person may mentally rehearse and edit what is to be said. When making a presentation in class or going to a job interview, for instance, then the conscious preparation for talking becomes similar to that of writing.

There are two distinctions to make with any type of communication. Talking or writing may be

- Low-stakes
- High-stakes

And it may

- Depend on context
- Stand alone

The first distinction relates to the sense of consequence for the communication. The more high-stakes something is, the more preparation is needed for it. Casual conversation is rarely high-stakes, whereas job interviews nearly always are. In regard to the second distinction, talking is always more contextual than writing, because it is possible to see how the other person(s) in the conversation are reacting. Similarly, some writing, such as instant messaging or texting, is contextual in that it has the benefit of immediate feedback. Much writing, however, particularly in academic environments, will stand alone. Other than low-stakes, contextual situations, most writing requires some planning. Even writing out a shopping list for another person requires some thought, as the writing must stand on its own without the ability to be clarified. You may reread the list to ensure that it is accurate and complete.

Writing for criminal justice, like all academic writing, improves as you know more about what you are doing. Even writing that seems relatively low-stakes, such as taking notes in a classroom, is potentially high-stakes if the notes become part of studying for an exam or writing a paper. Thus, planning and knowing when and how to take notes is important and can have an effect on the result (your grade in the class.) In order for the notes to be useful, it must be possible to take the notes out of the lecture and be able to understand and learn from the content.

Planning for criminal justice writing does not begin when you get an assignment, but much earlier. All communication occurs in a "rhetorical situation." In addition to the message, it involves:

- Persona (a communicator)
- An audience (the reader)
- A purpose (meaning of the message)

It is important to think about these things before beginning to write. From whose perspective are you trying to communicate a message? Who is the audience and what do they want? What are you trying to accomplish in writing this paper? What are you trying to say? In order to answer these questions, it is necessary to understand the rhetorical situation of criminal justice writing and then apply it to specific tasks. This includes understanding the persona, audience, and purpose.

PERSONA

An effect of any communication is recognition of the qualities of the communicator. In face-to-face communication, the listener is affected by how the communicator dresses, the body language, the tone of voice, and so forth. Though the recognition of personal qualities is less obvious in written communication, it is still true. For it to be effective, the written communication has to be seen as coming from someone who is interested, reliable, and trustworthy. The face that this writing presents to the reader is called the *persona*. The persona is a selection of characteristics of the writer that are appropriate to making the written communication effective. In other words, when you are writing, the image you portray to the reader is your persona.

It is best to begin thinking about the persona you wish to project first in terms of the course you are taking and then to refine that persona in terms of particular assignments. Much of the persona is tacit (unwritten, implied) and preexists the assignment. You could say that your persona is that of a "good student," except that the term is vague and therefore not very helpful. Walvoord and McCarthy (1990) suggest that the persona most valued by professors, in all cases, is a *professional-in-training*. A professional-in-training is someone who is working to join the academic conversation and community implied by the course—someone who values and uses the methods and knowledge provided by the course toward the course's goals.

Walvoord and McCarthy (1990) also explain the two least successful, and common, personae adopted by students: the *text processor* and the *layman*. The text processor does not adapt an effective persona, because he or she relies excessively on the textbook and other texts, thus failing to develop the necessary discipline-based independence the course demands. Alternatively, the layman has an excess of independence, and is either ignorant of or ignores the methodology and knowledge that the course provides. Often this distinction appears in tone of voice or point of view: a text processor sounds like a textbook and a layman like an editorial. The text processor and layman are both at dead ends: the text-processor cannot add to knowledge, because the text has already said what there is say; the layman will not add to knowledge, because he or she does not understand or value how knowledge is produced. The professional-in-training, on the other hand, knows how knowledge is produced and has the ability to advance beyond the textbook to produce it.

This persona is constructed from the beginning of the course. You want to learn to speak the language of the academic community you wish to join, to ask questions they value and provide answers arrived at in a way they will also value. When you enter a course, you want to achieve and help foster the goals of the course as they may have been stated on the syllabus, the course description in the catalog, the instructor's opening remarks, or implicitly in the course's activities. That is, if a goal of the course is that students learn to evaluate and reason from evidence, then your persona is someone who wishes to find relevant evidence and restrict conclusions to what the evidence supports. If a goal is to learn research methodology, then your persona is committed to the rigorous collection and testing of data. If a goal is to recognize and evaluate the spectrum of opinion on a topic, your persona—while committed to what you think is the best option—recognizes, respects, and can state fairly opposition stances. In other words, when you begin a course of study, you should try to become the kind of person who will do well in it, and then that persona will carry over into your writing assignments. The more you internalize the goals of the course, the easier the preparation for each part of it.

Examples of text processor, layman, and professional-in-training will help to illustrate the meaning of persona. If you are taking a class on the death penalty, you may be required to write a paper on the deterrent effects of capital punishment. The text processor would be able to recite information from texts and studies that show whether there is a deterrent effect. The writer with this persona would not, however, provide analysis of the issue. The layman may make comments such as, "I think that it is good to have the death penalty. I think more criminals should be put to death, like child molesters and drunk drivers." Although this statement elaborates upon the writer's opinion of the death penalty, it adds nothing factual to the topic and is simply subjective. The professional-in-training may begin the same way as the text processor, stating facts from books and articles on the topic of the death penalty. However, he or she would then elaborate on the facts and provide analysis, such as, "Although studies do not show that the death penalty has a deterrent effect, the methodology of these studies is questionable and the death penalty may have a deterrent effect for some people."

One chief reason for editing and proofreading the final draft of any written work before submitting it is that such editing (or lack of) reflects on the persona of the writer. Generally, readers are looking for content, not error. When obvious errors thrust themselves on the reader's consciousness, the reader is likely to wonder why the writer has not noticed or fixed them. If the reader suspects the writer of carelessness or indifference to grammatical or spelling mistakes, the reader may also suspect carelessness or indifference to the accuracy of the data or the rigor of the argument in the written work. On the other hand, freedom from writing error may suggest other higher-order competence. Though content and grammatical/spelling errors are not necessarily linked, the reader may perceive them to be, so it is worth your attention to edit carefully.

AUDIENCE

Part of preparing to write is recognizing and assessing your audience. Much of the academic writing done in school is never submitted to anyone and is, therefore, for yourself alone and for your own purposes. Examples are text and lecture notes, journals, and brainstorming for a paper.

These escape the ordinary audience constraints and should be judged largely on their usefulness to you, to help you master material or try out ideas. Once another person is the recipient, even if the recipient is a friend or a tutor, you have an obligation to recognize that person's knowledge and expectations, and to translate the intellectual shorthand that works well for self-communication into language that honors differences in thinking and knowledge. The conventions of communicating with others, and especially with others in the academic discipline, increasingly come into play as one moves up a hierarchy from personal, ungraded writing to graded writing for the professor. Remember to aim for the persona of professional-in-training. If you are writing for other students in the class, they, too, are professionals-in-training and have been instructed by the professor in how to maintain their roles while they read your writing. The professor, of course, is the professional and the representative of the discipline and the academic community you are joining. The professor is not just the recipient but also the judge of your communication. His or her judgment is representative of the wider community whose expectations the professor certifies you as having met.

In writing for criminal justice, more than for most other academic disciplines, the matter of audience is complicated by the requirement of role-playing, both for you and for the reader. For instance, you may be asked to be a lawyer writing for another lawyer or a judge, or as a police officer writing for the police chief. The role-playing will add additional constraints in terms of what the assumed audience expects and needs, but it is well to keep in mind a hierarchy of expectations. If your sense of what the role-playing requires seems to conflict with what you would deem to be proper academic writing, your priority should be to satisfy the professor's aim for the assignment and not role play. Lawyers, for example, sometimes succeed with illogical or emotional appeals, but professors will rarely accept such appeals from students.

As the primary audience for graded writing, the professor's chief expectation is that you will do the assignment. You need to know what that entails. Sometimes it is elaborately explained; often it is not. Even when the assignment has explicit instructions (i.e., it includes a list of specific points you must address), professors always have tacit expectations that are unstated. If you are not sure about the professor's expectation about the manuscript appearance (whether it should be single- or double-spaced, stapled or in a binder, etc.), you should find out and apportion your efforts accordingly. But those are surface concerns, and the tacit concerns are usually more significant. What are the expectations for how you will manage your content or how you will organize your material? Some assignments fall into recognizable *genres* or types, such as a book review. If you've done similar assignments in the past, you must be sure your professor shares the understanding of the genre you have already developed. A book review in the journal *Criminology* is unlikely to have the same features as a book report you wrote for high-school English. The second part of this book will try to help you with concerns related to specific assignments such as literature reviews.

Differing Attitudes Toward Student Writing

Professors of criminal justice courses are most often social scientists, though sometimes they are law enforcement or correctional professionals or lawyers. You should recognize that it is hard to generalize about what they want or expect and that even two professors with similar backgrounds and interests may differ considerably in what they seek from student writers. Still, some additional considerations may prove helpful. In particular, it is helpful to recognize that some of the criteria you may have become used to through other courses, such as subjective expressiveness, may not only no longer apply but actually be detrimental to good performance.

EXPRESSIVENESS

Some professors very much value authenticity, sincerity, and personal voice in papers. They want papers to express the real feelings and thoughts of the student in a voice that is authentically the student's. They see writing as part of the student's personal and intellectual development and are particularly looking for what is singular in the student's thought. At an extreme, some are even willing to countenance (or encourage) deviations from standard spelling or usage in the interest of maximum expressiveness.

Do not assume that a criminal justice professor values expressiveness. Some professors will be not only uninterested in but actively unreceptive toward expression of personal opinion, especially if your sole reason for including it is based on sincerity (e.g., "But I really believe that the death penalty is unconstitutional.") You are, of course, entitled to your own opinion, but if it is not actively solicited for the assignment, it is likely best not to state it. Additionally, in criminal justice assignments, you are responsible for any generalization you make and it must be fully supported by objective facts. Most criminal justice assignments are written in the third person rather than first person, thus avoiding the use of statements such as, "I believe," "I feel," and "in my opinion." When you make a statement summarizing facts, your opinion is assumed; you do not need to explicitly state that the sentence reflects your opinion. For instance, in a paper discussing the costs and benefits of capital punishment, you do not want to end the essay by saying, "Therefore, I believe that capital punishment should be abolished." Instead, you should state your opinion as "Based upon the above facts, capital punishment should be considered unconstitutional and should be abolished." There is no rule or fact stating that capital punishment should be abolished; therefore, the tacit implication is that you believe capital punishment should be abolished, and you base your opinion upon objective facts.

FORMAL CONSIDERATIONS

When grading, some professors take into consideration structural issues in addition to content. For these professors, a good essay must approximate a certain form, such as the five-paragraph essay, and the essay must not have errors in spelling and grammar. For criminal justice professors, such formal considerations are often necessary for a good grade, but these formal considerations tend to be of peripheral interest. That is, professors wish to receive correctly written and edited essays and will often specify length, paragraphing, reference format, and stylistic concerns and will reduce the grade for a paper if it fails to meet those criteria. However, their primary consideration is of the content. Assuming your writing is intelligible, criminal justice professors, like those in other disciplines, vary considerably in their interest in and tolerance for deviations from standard usage. It is always safest to be as correct as possible, but not everyone includes perfect grammar, spelling, and structure as a grading criterion. Lawyers, on the other hand, tend to be quite conservative on linguistic issues. As a general rule, writing assignments for criminal justice classes should never contain slang or abbreviated language, such as that used in text messaging (e.g., "If the police r in ur 'hood, it is bad.")

QUOTATION

Social scientists do use quotes, though sparingly. More often they summarize or paraphrase information from another source. An exception is that in legal writing, laws and judicial holdings regularly require exact quotation.

When you do use exact quotations in a criminal justice paper, there are a few important issues to consider. First, do not quote excessively. The aim of any criminal justice paper is to express your ideas, not those of other authors. Second, when you do quote another author, use only those words that are necessary to make your point. Although a criminal justice researcher may use a paragraph to explain an issue, you do not need to quote this entire paragraph in your essay. Third, if you do need to use a long quote, you need to use a specific format. Any quote over five lines long should be single-spaced and indented, and does not require quotation marks. It should, however, still be cited correctly, with the name of the author, year of the publication, and the page on which the quote occurred. Finally, when quoting (or paraphrasing information from) another author, it is very important to correctly attribute the information to the author. Anytime you use an exact phrase from another author, even if it is not a full sentence, you need to use quotation marks around that phrase. Otherwise, using another author's ideas is considered plagiarism. Referencing, a very important issue in criminal justice writing, is discussed at greater length in Chapter 9.

COVERAGE OF READING

The purpose of a high-school book report was to prove to the teacher that you had read the book, and that was usually accomplished by a summary of the book from beginning to end. In criminal justice college courses, some professors will assign a book review, ask you to review a journal article, or ask you to review a series of articles and books (called a literature review). Though coverage of the material remains important, most professors who require such assignments do not want a simple summary, or *description,* of the contents you read. Instead, the professor is most likely seeking a *critical analysis* of the main issue in the reading(s). Rather than simply describe the issue, you should identify the main issue in the reading and carefully evaluate its significance. This evaluation includes a brief description, often coupled with a discussion of the costs and benefits of the issue. It may require that you compare and contrast the issues with other sources. Though it may be acceptable for you to include in the assignment a discussion of why the reading was (or was not) beneficial to you, it is more important to discuss whom in the criminal justice field this book would most benefit.

"CREATIVE" WRITING

Professors in some disciplines encourage students to develop an eccentric or entertaining prose style, marked by such things as puns, metaphors, or similes that are sufficiently far-fetched or extended to call attention to themselves. This may include unusually erudite or colloquial vocabulary, such informal punctuation as dashes and exclamation marks, and the artistic use of fragments or comma splices. Although criminal justice is not to be reduced to the "just the facts ma'am" of the old *Dragnet* show, it very much favors a factual, objective prose style. This is not to say that you want to try for a dull prose. A precise diction and sentence structure that emphasizes meaning or the shape of thought is critical and will allow you to clearly state the key points of your argument.

PURPOSE

The third part of the rhetorical situation, in addition to persona and audience, is the writer's purpose in the written assignment. Purpose refers to what the writer is primarily trying to accomplish in the writing. There is an interdependence of purpose with audience and persona. A writer who wants to persuade will try to project a fair-minded persona so that the audience will trust what he or she writes. The writer will want the audience to share the writing's purpose (for instance, the writer will write and the audience will read with the same desire to clarify an issue).

The persona or the writer's sense of the audience often appears through the writer's explicit statements (for instance, if the purpose is an objective evaluation of the death penalty case law, the writer must state so in the thesis).

Your notion of purpose may be either fairly simple or more elaborate. The writer may be an intermediary between authorities (or sources) and data (or the world of fact) on the one hand, and the audience on the other, with the writer's purpose toward the audience to use the sources and facts either to inform, to persuade or both. The broad category of "inform," however, may involve different behaviors and results. Inform may mean to:

- Clarify
- Illustrate or exemplify
- Explain
- Narrate
- Describe
- Compare
- Define
- Classify
- Analyze
- Review
- Summarize

All of these will inform the reader but involve different behavior from the writer, which will alter how the reader is informed. "Persuade" can similarly be differentiated, and it can mean to:

- Propose
- Evaluate
- Critique
- Refute

The professor may either explicitly state or imply what the purpose is in an assignment. Part of the student's job in conceiving the assignment is to decide what its purpose is, and part of the job of achieving the finished product is to make that purpose either explicit or clearly implicit to the audience.

It is important to recognize that there are many purposes to writing that may not hold for academic or criminal justice writing. Writers in the media often write to entertain, celebrate, commemorate, or preach; academic writers do not regard any of these as primary purposes and most likely do not attempt to accomplish them. Similarly, academic writing does not have as its primary purpose to shock, horrify, or titillate, and generally tries to avoid such outcomes. Yet some of what the writer is being informative about may shock, horrify, or titillate, particularly with the use of examples to clarify a point, as long as there appears to be no obvious manipulation to do so. Moreover, *pathos* (appeals to the audience's fear, anger, or pity) is a recognized aspect of persuasion, though it is effective only if strictly subordinated to logical argument. For instance, if the purpose of the paper is to discuss the utility of death penalty, the writer can elaborate upon violent, premeditated murders in order to emphasize the focus of the laws. Emotional appeal is particularly effective if one is trying to motivate behavior, but remember that in academic writing one is only theoretically trying to motivate behavior, and is actually writing an assignment.

PUTTING PERSONA, AUDIENCE, AND PURPOSE TOGETHER: AN EXAMPLE

In order to understand how persona, audience, and purpose play a role in a criminal justice writing course, it is helpful to look at a sample assignment. The course is "Sex Offenders in the Criminal Justice System." The writing assignment is as follows:

> Write a letter to a state legislator from the perspective of a victim of a sexual offense. The letter should be about five pages and should include the following information: what you went through as a victim; your experience with law enforcement officers and in the court process; problems with these processes and what should be changed; how you feel now towards the offender; and how you would feel if he or she were released from prison. Use at least three sources that were not part of required reading for the course.

Persona

You are writing from the perspective of a victim of sexual abuse, but you need to remember at all times that you are really writing as a student in the course. An actual victim writing a letter might express anger, hurt, shame, embarrassment, and fear, and might also write in graphic language with little editing or proofreading. The audience of a "state legislator" is meant to make the writing a piece of public prose presented with appropriate demeanor and care, even though only some victims would be guided accordingly. But this is an academic assignment, and you should be very careful about deviations from conventions of academic prose for the sake of sounding more realistically like a victim. Most importantly, an actual victim is a *layman*, working from personal experience and knowing only what a victim knows. You, on the other hand, are a *professional-in-training*, so you also know and will use material from three sources and from the course you have been taking. Balancing your two roles of victim and professional-in-training should keep you from being a mere *text processor*, who simply relays what the sources say. As a victim, you need to use the sources as part of what looks like a personal statement.

In order to better understand the aims of the course and the perspective sought by the professor, it will help to look at the stated course objectives. These read:

> The aim of this course is to develop an understanding of the causes of sexual offending and how sex offenders are handled throughout the criminal justice system. Sex offenders constitute a heterogeneous group of individuals, and this course examines all categories of those labeled as sex offenders. There is an analysis of the laws that relate to sex offenders, particularly Megan's Law, sexually violent predator (SVP) laws, and residency restrictions. There is an analysis of the difficulty in balancing rights of the offenders and rights of the community, and what forms of community protection are viable for these offenders. By the end of the course, students should have an understanding of sex offender typologies, types of treatment offered to sex offenders, laws and policies regarding sex offenders, the impact of sexual victimization, and the likely future direction of sex offender legislation.

What does this statement suggest about the persona of a writer in the course that might influence how the assignment is conceived? Because the letter is to a state legislator, it suggests a writer with a lively and informed interest in "the likely future direction of legislation." The legislator will be interested in the victim's information and conclusions about problems in the law enforcement and court processes, because the legislator must evaluate current legislation regulating these processes. The legislator is interested in how the victim feels about the offender, especially about the possible release of the offender, because punishment of offenders and community protection are also the subject of legislation. Unlike an ordinary victim, who may know only his or her attacker, the student has learned about "sex offender typologies." Unlike the ordinary victim, who only wants his or her wishes translated to law, the student knows about existing law and can make informed choices about what will really aid the victim. Although the student should not write as if angry, embarrassed, hurt, and shamed, he or she should acknowledge that a victim would have those feelings and express them in the essay.

Notice in particular the phrase about "balancing rights of the offenders and rights of the community." A victim might not only be indifferent but actively hostile to offenders' rights, but the student who must balance rights is expected to champion the victim within the context of accepted offender rights.

Audience

The audience for the letter is twofold: the legislator, who is the theoretical audience as suggested by the assignment, and the professor, who will be grading the assignment. The state legislator and the professor have much in common in expecting good writing and an objective tone. In order for a legislator to evaluate the current laws, the victim must provide him or her with objective facts regarding problems in the criminal justice system, based upon those faced by the victim. The legislator would be concerned about what is wrong with the current law, why it should be changed, and how the change can be accomplished.

In addition to these issues, the professor has formal concerns, unlike the legislator, such as with the use and proper documentation of sources. Although a real victim would have his or her personal experience to draw upon, the professor is expecting the student to draw upon the source material or material previously available in the course to construct a victim experience or an offender profile that is interesting and plausible. The professor-as-audience will then evaluate the choices the student makes in these areas. Another important note is that the professor would require that the student recognize the legislator as his or her audience. As such, the professor would expect the student to be aware of what legislators do and the concerns that legislators face (e.g., balancing the rights of offenders and the community.) Thus, throughout the writing assignment, the student must remember to write to the audience of both professor and legislator.

Purpose

The assignment has several purposes, as described by the different tasks outlined. The first purpose is to provide information (e.g., what you as a victim went through, your experience, how you feel). The next purpose of the essay is to persuade the legislator of necessary changes in the law. A novice writer might treat each task as a separate essay, in which case the letter would be predominantly informative. However, recognition that the audience is a legislator would suggest that the primary purpose of the letter is to influence legislation. Therefore, the informative parts, though some of them may exist for their own sake, should largely exist to lead to policy recommendations, and the recommendations should have a solid foundation in the objective facts of the essay. In other words, the informative part of the assignment should be minimal, but the information you provide here is crucial to create sound recommendations. The professor obviously wants the student to show mastery of both the source and course material and an ability to integrate them into both credible narrative of the victim's experiences and recommendations that are responsive to existing and recommended legislation. Without forsaking the victim's side or perspective, the essay should show an academic judiciousness.

Summary

When writing a criminal justice assignment, it is important to understand the rhetorical situation, or what you need to communicate, to whom, and how persuasively. In order to fully understand the rhetorical situation, you should identify three components in each assignment: the persona the professor expects you to adopt, the audience to whom you are writing, and the purpose of the assignment. Although you are a student and will therefore always be writing to the professor as your audience, criminal justice assignments often require that you also write to a "theoretical" audience, such as a legislator, a judge, an offender, or a victim. Though it is always important to consider the formal structure of the writing assignment, the most important aspect of a criminal justice paper is the content. Thus, remember from which perspective you are writing, to whom, and what you are trying to accomplish.

Reference

Walvoord, B. E. & McCarthy, L. P. (1990). *Thinking and writing in college: A naturalistic study of students in four disciplines.* Urbana, IL: NTCE.

3 | THE **WRITING** PROCESS

You may have read a chapter on the writing process in an introductory composition class, but the writing process described in this chapter is quite different. It will have the same purpose of preparing you to write, but it will be geared specifically towards the writing process in the criminal justice discipline. What can be said about the writing process in general has limited use, both for you personally and for writing about criminal justice. There is no single writing process, but rather writing processes.

The most important thing for you to do is to accept that you are a writer, that you are going to continue to be one while you are in school, and that you will most likely continue to write in some capacity throughout your career. Writing is not all you will do, but it is a significant part of criminal justice classes and careers, and you need to take yourself seriously as a writer. This is true whether you become a police officer (writing reports), a lawyer (writing legal briefs), a probation officer (writing field notes and reports), or any other criminal justice professional. All advice about writing and the writing process must be personalized to fit you. Take note of your environment when you write and the way in which you do it. Do you need quiet, music, or ordinary noise? How comfortable are you composing on a computer? Are you more comfortable writing first with a pen and paper? Do you work in short or long bursts? How much do you compose in your head? Do you write quickly or slowly? Do you write easily or painfully? If you walk around composing in your head and commit to writing only after you have mentally shaped what you want, advice to try free writing will not work for you. Though your own process is not inevitable and may be improved, improvement may not come from going against your natural bent.

What do you want out of your criminal justice class and your writing career? Economist Herbert Simon coined the word *satisfice* to mean trying to do not the best possible job, but rather to do a job good enough to get by and move on. All college students satisfice sometimes. Your writing process will depend on your motivation. This book largely assumes that you want to do your best and will prefer more elaborate processes that will help you (though it will also help those who want to satisfice only).

This book also works under the assumption that you have enough of an interest in the course to put on, for the short term (a semester) or for the long term (throughout your career), the role of professional-in-training discussed under *persona* in Chapter 2. That is what your teacher expects and what students who are motivated, or those who want to do more than satisfice, do. Your thinking and writing processes then will include not only what you do for a particular assignment but also what you use from your previous education and what you do to further that education past the assignment. Much of this book will be about showing you how to accomplish specific tasks set out by your professors, but it is important that you aim to achieve long-term goals. You are in charge of your education; writing assignments should do more than get good grades. They should help you become the criminal justice professional you want to be by furthering your interests as well as establishing competence in the course.

PREVIOUS KNOWLEDGE

It is important to recognize that your mind is not a blank slate. Most writing assignments will draw on what you already know, in addition to what you are specifically asked to research. Your previous knowledge includes:

- *Knowledge and thinking about criminal justice.* As outlined in Chapter 1 (Box 1.1), criminal justice issues appear so frequently in the news, reading, and conversation that you probably already know many things about the topic. Some of this knowledge is erroneous; for instance, crime dramas on television indicate that the investigative and adjudication processes happen in a timely fashion (an hour!), yet the reality is that they often take years. However, those same shows may teach the viewers about diverse issues such as DNA, the role of the police, the structure of a courtroom, and so forth. In addition to this peripheral knowledge, some students (or their friends or family members) will have had personal experience with the criminal justice system, which would also add to prior knowledge.
- *Academic knowledge.* Before beginning a writing assignment for a particular class, you will have learned information in that class that is relevant to the assignment. Additionally, if you have taken previous courses in the field of criminal justice, that information is also probably applicable. Even if you have not taken criminal justice courses, you can also apply information you learned in other disciplines such as sociology, psychology, law, history, and anthropology.
- *Repertoire of problem-solving and writing experiences and strategies.* You have been developing writing, reading, thinking, and problem-solving skills since you began your education. Though criminal justice courses may require additional knowledge in these areas, you should have some sense of how to go about accomplishing these goals.
- *Assessment of the rhetorical situation.* By the time you enter college, you have most likely previously constructed a writing persona, anticipated an audience response, and recognized purposes to your writing. Although any assignment creates its own rhetorical situation, as discussed in Chapter 2, your previous experience should also assist you in understanding how to create this for a criminal justice writing assignment.
- *Tacit knowledge of the discourse community.* You should understand the discourse community of criminal justice professionals that you aspire to join. You may know what interests it; what it values; the conventions of producing and communicating knowledge to which it subscribes; and what it counts and does not count as evidence, proof, or argument. You can take this knowledge and apply it to the writing task at hand.

THE WRITING PROCESS: LINEAR OR RECURSIVE?

Textbooks often divide the writing process into three parts or stages, variously named (1) prewriting, writing, and rewriting, or (2) planning, drafting, and editing. This book accepts that such a structure will exist in criminal justice writing as well, as nearly everyone thinks before writing, if only for a few seconds, and many look over what they have written, if only as cursory proofreading. However, the book will expand on these stages, which assume that the writing process is structured linearly. It is a mistake to think that planning ends when writing begins, and that editing occurs only after writing ends. Though this may be the case some-times, with particularly easy assignments, writing is more often recursive, or these stages continue repeatedly. You think through the problem, begin to write a draft, discover that you need to do more preparing, draft again, evaluate what you have written, and redraft. The linear structure of planning, drafting, and editing is too rigid and may lead to ideas that are not fully developed. Moreover, if you feel you must know everything you are going to say before you start drafting, you may find yourself unable to begin or progress. A more fluid sense of the writing process allows you to start drafting with the thought that writing will spur you to further thinking.

Another way to enhance the criminal justice writing process is to think of it as a "cognitive process." This way of looking at writing stems from work done by Linda Flowers and John Hayes and colleagues at Carnegie-Mellon. Flower and Hayes (1977) regard writing as a species of problem solving. It is useful to think of a problem as involving *goals, strategies,* and *tests. Goals* are where you want to go; *strategies* are your means of getting there; *tests* are your means of assessing whether you have gotten there. In terms of the writing process, one might think that articulating goals and choosing reading, thinking, and drafting strategies to achieve those goals might be part of the prewriting or planning stage, and testing the draft to see whether it has accomplished the goals might be part of the rewriting stage. That is true; however, these do not always occur linearly. What makes the writing process recursive is the need to refine or change goals after the writing has begun, discovering more effective strategies along the way, and changing tests to reflect the changed goals. Therefore, rather than thinking of the writing process as having three distinct stages, think of it as consisting of constantly evolving goals, strategies, and tests.

APPLYING THE WRITING PROCESS TO AN ASSIGNMENT

What happens when we get an assignment? It will help to begin with one. The following assignment is from the course "Sexual Offenders in the Criminal Justice System."

> You will be required to write a report and give a presentation on Megan's Law. Each person will be assigned a different state to research and given specific questions to answer on that state. You will use the Internet to find the registration and notification requirements for the state you were assigned, and also explain whether the state has passed sexually violent predator legislation. You will give a brief presentation on what the state requirements are and your opinion of those requirements. This assignment will be between five and ten pages long, depending on the state you choose. This assignment is worth 30 percent of the grade and is due in one month.

Time and Effort

The first thing you should do is consider the weight of the assignment. In this case, you can look at three factors to tell you how much effort to put into the assignment: how much of your grade it is worth, the type of work it entails, and the amount of time given to complete the assignment. Worth 30 percent of your grade, this is a significant assignment for the course. Even if the syllabus calls for an additional assignment of this magnitude, you should expect to put in hard work on an assignment worth this much of your grade. You should also note that it requires multiple tasks; not only do you need to hand in a five- to ten-page report, but you also need to give an oral presentation. Additionally, the assignment states that you will be required to do two types of research: research on registration and notification laws, and research on sexually violent predator legislation. This quantity of research will require a significant amount of time. Finally, the assignment notes that you have a month to complete the assignment, which is another indicator of the teacher's expectation of the level of effort you must show. Taken together, it should be clear that this is not an assignment that can be done overnight, and it will require a significant level of research, time, and effort.

Tasks

The syllabus states that the assignment will involve two tasks: research into the registration and notification laws and research about sexually violent predator legislation in a particular state. It is likely that students know several pieces of information about this assignment going into the class. They probably know something about sex offenders, because many news reports and television shows discuss issues related to them. Students may not fully understand correct facts related to sex offenders, however. For instance, before taking the class they may not know that sex offenders have a lower recidivism (or reoffending) rate than any other type of violent offender except for murderers, and that 90 percent of victims know their abusers. The students are likely to learn about this information from the readings and lectures in the course. Students are also likely to know something about Megan's Law going into the class, because it is a topic that has been discussed in the news over the last decade. The specifics of the law, as well as why this and other sexually violent predator legislation were implemented, can be learned from the lectures and the readings. The main focus of the research for this assignment then will be to determine how these laws apply to a particular state. If, for example, you are assigned the state of North Dakota, you will have to do research to find out about North Dakota's Megan's Law.

In addition to researching the facts about these issues, the assignment also asks for your opinion of the laws. If you simply locate and report facts, and then respond briefly and generally with your opinion (e.g., approving of the legislation without explaining why), you will miss an important aspect of the assignment. If the professor wants only the facts, the professor will ask for only objective research. Though it is important to include the objective facts, or what the laws state, it is just as important to subjectively analyze the laws and explain why you do or do not support them. The professor is asking for you to evaluate the objective facts, and your grade will be based partially on how well you analyze the facts and how well you can support your position.

It is helpful to keep in mind that you are learning these facts to enter into a disciplinary conversation. Your knowledge of the discipline tells you that laws are implemented to control or alter people's behavior, and your previous knowledge and the knowledge gained from the course tells you that stopping sexual predators and protecting children are primary goals of Megan's Law. You should also know, based on prior knowledge, disciplinary knowledge, and knowledge from the course, that criminal laws must balance the rights of the community (community protection) and the rights of the offenders (constitutional protections). Because Megan's Law treats one group of offenders differently than others, has applied laws *ex post facto,* and may socially stigmatize those who are required to register, but at the same time also informs the community of potentially dangerous predators, does it balance the rights of the community and the offenders?

Having this disciplinary knowledge allows you to see that your opinion may deal with one or both of these two questions: are the laws likely to work? Is the legal treatment of offenders fair? To respond fully, you should be able to state your opinion and support it with facts from the literature. For instance, you may state that although there are no research studies that show Megan's Law reduces recidivism in sex offenders, studies on supervision and management of sex offenders indicate that enhanced supervision reduces recidivism. Therefore, you support Megan's Law because it provides enhanced supervision of sex offenders in the community. You could also point out that although Megan's Law appears to violate the individual rights of the offenders, courts across the country, including the U.S. Supreme Court, have declared that the laws are constitutional because they are not punitive but rather regulatory.

Note the need for recursive activity in this assignment. As you begin to think about the second part of the assignment, the statement of your opinion, you may find yourselves modifying your original goals and tasks. You begin the assignment by stating the facts of the law in your state. It is clear, based upon the way the syllabus states the assignment, that states have varying laws related to the registration and notification of sex offenders. To provide a thorough opinion of the issue, it would be helpful for you to understand states' registration and notification laws for purposes of contrast. What are the similarities and differences, and what effect does this have on the way that the law is enforced? It may be helpful to find out about the expressed intentions of the legislators or public reaction to the laws. In summary, you should not think that the research for this assignment is going to be limited to the relatively simple task of discovering your state's laws, or you will subsequently find that you need to do additional research.

GOALS OF THE ASSIGNMENT

There are two parts to the assignment used in the sample here, and each part of the assignment has different goals. The goal of the first part of the assignment, which involves researching and reporting the facts of the laws, is straightforward: it is to represent the facts accurately and thoroughly. The goal of the second part of the assignment, involving the expression of your opinion about the laws, is more ambiguous. It is possible to identify different types of goals in this second part of the assignment: the professor's goals and your own. The professor's goals, if not explicit in the assignment, come from the course. What has the professor emphasized throughout the semester? For instance, has the professor emphasized the need for community protection from sexual predators? If so, your opinion should address this issue, whichever way your support falls. Next, what about Megan's Law interests you? Perhaps you are interested in enforceability issues. For instance, how can the state enforce registration and notification of homeless sex offenders? How does each jurisdiction have the resources to track all sex offenders? How can the state ensure that sex offenders are not committing offenses in jurisdictions where they are not registered? The opinion section of the assignment should reflect your consideration of both the professor's and your goals.

Format

Related to deciding goals for the assignment is a preliminary sense of what format, or what sections, the written assignment might have. Most assignments should begin with an introductory paragraph or section. The introduction should state the thesis of the essay, or the main points that you will address, and should establish a context for the assignment within the disciplinary conversation. Subsequent to the introduction, the assignment calls for at least two sections in the body of the text: one reporting the facts and the other expressing your opinion. Finally, you should summarize the key issues from the paper in a conclusion.

Planning

Part of deciding what to do is deciding the order in which to do it. There is a necessary order for certain tasks in this project. For instance, you must learn the facts about the laws before you can state an opinion of the laws, and thus you must conduct the research to obtain the facts before beginning the analysis. A good place to begin the research is by reviewing the syllabus. If there are readings on the syllabus in connection with the assignment, it would be helpful to read them in advance to help establish the context necessary for the research. The sooner you complete the readings on the syllabus, the better, as you will also need to make time to do Internet research, possibly further readings from the library, and the analysis for the project. If you have your own computer and access to the Internet, you should not have as much difficulty scheduling time to conduct the Internet research or search for library books. However, if you need to use a computer at your college, make sure to schedule enough time to thoroughly research the topics.

Before beginning the drafting of the assignment, you need to plan the drafting. One possibility is to wait to begin drafting until you have finished all the reading, research, and analysis. Alternatively, you may be more comfortable drafting the assignment in stages. Either way, it would be helpful to first draft an outline of the project to lay out the key ideas that you plan to write about. The final version of the introduction is likely to be the last thing you complete; however, an early, tentative introduction is helpful in establishing what issues you intend to present. Imagining the context of the assignment at the outset by putting it in writing will assist you with the research and analysis. When you begin drafting the assignment, you will discover further questions or gaps in your research or thinking. Evaluation throughout the drafting stage will become an aid to research, discovery, and further drafting, and you need to manage your time to allow for this evaluation process.

Reading, Note-Taking and Thinking

Once you have established goals, assessed what tasks you must perform to achieve the goals of the assignment, and determined how long the assignment may take to complete, you need to begin the reading, note-taking, and thinking in order to prepare to draft the assignment.

Taking notes on what you read is an important part of the process of writing with research, and it can be a complex task. Note-taking changes, depending on:

- The stage of the thinking and writing process
- Whether you are (mostly) researching from a computer or from books and articles
- Your comfort level with older (index card) or newer (data base) techniques
- Your changing purposes

Remember that writing is a recursive process. How and why you take notes will differ depending on what you are taking notes for and when you are taking them. Reading and taking notes for an assignment should be more focused than note-taking for a class. Unlike in a classroom, where you are hearing information for the first time, with an assignment you know what questions you need to answer and what information will help contribute to this answer. Not everything you read will lead to note-taking. When you are searching for a topic or when you are seeking to re-fine a topic to the point where it becomes manageable, it may be too soon to take notes. You are reading to get a sense of what is out there, and you will only impede the reading or browsing process if you feel that you have to take notes. Much of what you read may prove to be too gen-eral for your eventual topic or for some topic you decide against treating. Once you know what you are doing, you can always go back and take notes. Think of reading a corrections text, for ex-ample, as shopping in a department store without being ready to buy yet. Once you have a bet-ter idea of what you want, you can return to the relevant department; or, in the case of reading in corrections, you can concentrate more on characteristics of offenders and less on guards or alternative means of punishment.

The further along you are in the writing process, the more specific a sense you will have of what you are taking notes for. At the beginning, you may not be sure just what notes will be use-ful or just what use they will have, and you will surely amass more material than you need. At the end, if drafting or evaluating causes you to go back to research, you will likely be looking for something quite specific to fill a recognized gap and will take notes only when you find what you seek. If you are looking into the effect of religious conversion on convicts, it may be later in the process that you realize you should read and take notes about the religions to which offenders have converted.

One way of thinking about note-taking is by considering whether you have created an outline for the paper yet. Once you have an outline, and the more specific the headings in the outline are, the more purposive your note-taking will be. The outline, in effect, asks specific questions that will be answered based on your notes. Prior notes may help you formulate the question and provide a piece of the answer. Questions may alter the relevance or importance of some notes. If you discover that you do not have notes to cover a section, you must do further research. If, when you evaluate your notes, they do not seem good enough, then again you must do further research.

Another way of thinking about the same thing is that as you focus your topic, you will also focus your reading. You will be looking for articles that are more germane to your specific re-search problem or to specific aspects of it. Once you zero in on these most useful sources, the pro-portion of note-taking to reading will grow as you find a higher percentage of what you read worth taking notes on. In a later stage, when you already have most of what you need, you will be scanning sources just to fill a gap and you will once again be reading more than taking notes, al-though reading much more selectively than earlier.

HANDWRITING VERSUS WRITING ON A COMPUTER

There are two primary ways in which students take notes: writing them by hand or writing notes directly into a computer. Professors today require students to submit papers that are typed, and many students begin the writing process directly on the computer. However, remember that writ-ing on paper may be useful. If you do so, you should consider writing on index cards, which has the following advantages:

- The small size of index cards encourages students to identify only the most important in-formation, or at most a few related facts, on a card, thereby facilitating arrangement.
- The small space discourages quotation, especially long quotations, and encourages students to paraphrase or succinctly summarize.

- Colored index cards could be used to differentiate topics, or they could be used as bibliography cards, with only author's last name, date of source, and page at the bottom of the research card.

The use of the computer for the storage, retrieval, manipulation, and arrangement of research has altered the way most people work today. Now students may get much (if not all) of the research material needed online and simply download and copy points of interest. You can cut and paste material from one file to another, search for key words, use spell check and grammar functions, and so forth. Some programs (such as EndNote) will automatically alphabetize each bibliographic entry as you add to your bibliography and format it for you (such as in APA format), and with all the information from a single source in a single place, at least initially, you are less likely to find yourself with unidentified material.

On the other hand, there are drawbacks to taking notes on a computer. The ease of downloading encourages you to amass much more material, thereby making it more difficult to summarize sources succinctly as you write the assignment. Also, the material amassed is all in one source. Where a paraphrase requires you to select what you want and, in putting it in your language, both facilitates your understanding of the material and your manipulation of it for your own purpose, the block quoting you get from copying the material into your computer file lacks focus, postpones the task of understanding what is written, and exists to serve the source's purpose rather than yours. In other words, some of the ease of downloading and copying material is deceptive: you are only postponing the work of understanding, selection, and paraphrasing that someone writing by hand had to do up front.

Inexperienced writers may be tempted or trapped by the ease of computer use to commit research sins. Social science papers minimize, if not eliminate, quotation, whereas the availability of all that quoted material encourages it. Worse, one may fail to acknowledge an original data source and so plagiarize. Quotations, paraphrasing, and summarizing material from another source must be attributable to the author that wrote the material. Otherwise, this is plagiarism.

One trick to minimizing the disadvantages to computer use is to—either as you take notes or as soon as you review them—begin the process of selection, focus, and paraphrase. Just downloading material provides no mastery. Reading, paraphrasing, sorting, labeling, and rearranging it provide the mastery you need if you are going to own it. Cutting and pasting, where you dislodge material from its source and transfer it to a file that indicates your possible use of the material, is part of owning it. It is important, however, that you do not lose the citation when you cut and paste.

CITATIONS

One of the most important aspects of note-taking is its responsibility to honest and accurate citation of used material. Because your final paper will feature in-text citations and a reference list at the end of the paper in some format (such as APA, ASA, or MLA, as seen in Chapter 9), it is best to anticipate those needs in the note-taking process. Most people start keeping a working bibliography as soon as they start reading for the paper. The working bibliography lists not just what you are reading, but also what you decide you may subsequently want to read. If a source makes heavy use of another source, or suggests that another source would prove helpful, you make note of it on your working bibliography. If you are keeping notes on a computer, it is easy to alphabetize the list as you add to it, and you may even have a program that will automatically put the bibliographic information in the format you will need for the finished list. Bibliographic information includes the names of all authors (APA uses only initials for the first and middle names), title of article, title of book, date of publication, place of publication (for a book), volume and specific pages (for an article), and the website for online material. The first use of this information is to help you find what you are looking for; then you need to give your reader the same opportunity. Citations are discussed in more detail in Chapter 9.

Still, a working bibliography will be longer than the reference list you include at the end of your article. Unless told otherwise, insert on the final reference list only sources you have cited in the paper. Every source cited in the paper must be included in the reference list. That means you prepare the reference list from the working bibliography by deleting everything you did not end up citing in the text.

INTEGRATING SOURCE MATERIAL WITH YOUR OWN THINKING

Before you begin to integrate the notes into a paper, it is important to begin the thinking process. To begin thinking about the topic, you might want to use a "heuristic device" to stimulate the thought processes. For instance, focused free writing involves setting an alarm clock for about five minutes. Begin writing down everything you know or think about the topic. You are not allowed to stop or pause until the five-minute alarm goes off. You may not stop to read anything you are writing or cross anything out. Just keep writing: even if you think you have run out of things to say, you will find more simply from the pressure of needing to keep on writing. Most people will generate a significant amount of material in the time limit, much of it useful. This is an effective way of understanding at the outset what you know, and, more importantly, what you need to learn about the topic. Another example of a heuristic device is a topic tree, a more focused version of the focused free writing. Here you write a topic, like "importance of sex offender registration," in the middle of a page and circle it. Then you draw lines connecting parts of the topic to it, such as "community protection." As you do that, you may branch into more specifics for each part, such as "knowledge of sex offenders' whereabouts" under "community protection." These and other techniques will help you generate and recognize material.

It is important to distinguish your thoughts from your source; you should not confuse putting things into your own words with quoting or near-quoting. In criminal justice writing, you most often simply refer to a source for its findings or conclusions, which you put in your own words. But when you take notes, you don't yet know how you are going to use the source and therefore take more notes than you will use. Your notes may be paraphrasing or quoting even if the use in your final paper will be neither. You must know whether you are quoting, paraphrasing, or just summarizing.

One way to begin the integration of source material with your own thinking is to begin to draft parts of the paper. How soon you begin to draft and whether you are comfortable drafting isolated pieces of the paper may depend on both your own preferences for a writing process and your comfort level or sense of competence with the topic at the time you consider drafting.

DRAFTING

Though you have been taking notes already, note-taking differs from drafting. "Drafting" refers to writing the preliminary version of the assignment. Drafting will incorporate material from the notes you have taken, but these notes may be rewritten to fit the context of the draft. Drafting will eventually lead to a completed document, albeit one that will require editing and revising.

At what point you begin drafting depends upon how you like to work. Some students write one complete draft; others prefer to write several more tentative drafts of the assignment. The more preliminary or tentative a draft is, the sooner you will begin to draft and the faster you will complete it. Preliminary drafts are useful in outlining an organizational strategy for the paper. They are similar to notes, in that you do not yet need to be concerned with exactness of diction or correctness of grammar or spelling; these are the focus during the editing stage of the writing process. The key to the drafting stage is to outline a structure for the assignment, incorporate your research and notes, and identify where there are gaps in the research and writing.

Where to Start

The first thing to do is create an outline. Outlining the assignment is essential to understanding the structure of the assignment and identifying the sections. You know you will have at least three sections: an introduction, a body, and a conclusion. You also know that the body will have at least two sections: the facts and your opinion. You could break this down further and make three sections in the body: the facts of Megan's Law, the facts of sexually violent predator legislation, and your opinion. Taking this into consideration, an outline of this assignment might be as follows:

I. Introduction
II. Megan's Law
    A. What is it? Describe the inception of the law, and its goals and aims.
    B. What is Megan's Law in North Dakota?
    C. Court challenges to Megan's Law in North Dakota
III. Sexually violent predator (SVP) legislation
    A. What is it? Describe the law, and its goals and aims
    B. Describe SVP legislation in North Dakota, when this law was enacted, and why
    C. Court challenges to SVP legislation
IV. My opinion of the legislation
    A. Megan's Law
        1. No research shows that it prevents cases of sexual abuse
        2. It labels offenders; according to labeling theory, this may lead the offenders to commit more acts of sexual abuse, not deter them from future offenses (particularly juveniles)
        3. It does not adequately track offenders who are homeless, whose offenses are not reported, who are acquitted
        4. It does allow for quicker apprehension of repeat sex offenders
    B. SVP legislation
        1. Good if it focuses on the most serious sex offenders who could be a danger in the community
        2. There need to be protections in place to ensure that offenders can be treated, rehabilitated and released; this shouldn't be a substitute for prison
V. Conclusion

Note that Part IV of this outline represents an advanced stage of your thinking about the laws. You could still have a Part IV even if your thinking had not gone so far:

I. My opinion of the legislation
    A. Megan's Law
        1. What it does successfully

2. What it fails to do
3. Its success or failure on balance

B. SVP legislation
1. Its successes
2. Its drawbacks

Once you have this outline, you can begin to draft the paper.

THE INTRODUCTION

Introductions have several purposes, all useful not only for the reader's understanding of what is to follow, but also to remind the writer of what he or she is doing. Drafting an introduction helps the writer assess the level of understanding of the assignment and should address the following issues:

- *Context.* The introduction explains why the essay is being written. In the case of this assignment, the introduction states the value of looking into Megan's Law and sexually violent predator legislation of North Dakota. Why is it necessary to analyze these laws? What issues are you addressing? The context may suggest what questions you will answer or questions you plan to return to in the conclusion for a more thorough restatement.

- *The thesis statement.* The introduction should tell the reader, in a sentence, the main point of the essay. This is called the *thesis statement*. It makes a promise about what the reader should expect in the essay. It is important that the information in the essay explains fully the thesis statement and does not contradict it. The thesis statement is likely to be the last sentence modified in the revision process, as it must accurately reflect the information provided in the essay. An example of a thesis statement could be: "Though legislation related to convicted sex offenders is inherently flawed because of the underreporting of sexual offenses, North Dakota's versions of Megan's Law and sexually violent predator legislation are as well-conceived as those in any other state and should assist in the investigation of, if not the prevention of, sexual offenses."

- *Outline of the shape of the paper.* The introduction is where the writer can outline the organization of the paper and explain how the topics will develop. This is where the writer can describe what the sections of the paper are, the logic of the organization of the sections, and how the sections are linked. Think of the introduction as a "roadmap" to the rest of the paper. Be careful not to simply make a list of upcoming tasks (e.g., "First I am going to talk about Megan's Law in North Dakota. Then I will talk about the benefits and problems with Megan's Law"). Instead, explain the key issues that are going to be included in paper (e.g., "Varying versions of Megan's Law have been implemented in all fifty states, and this paper outlines the regulations for, benefits of, and problems with Megan's Law in North Dakota").

- *Methodology.* Methodology refers to the means, technique, or procedure used to answer a set of questions. In other words, it explains how the writer went about answering the questions asked in the assignment and assures the reader that the questions have been answered fully in a systemic manner. For assignments where the methodology is elaborate, the writer should give details as to how the key questions in the paper were answered. In some essays, such as the sample assignment given in this chapter, the methodology may be too straightforward to require more than a sentence or two of explanation. For instance, you could note in the introduction that information on Megan's Law and sexually violent predator legislation is readily available for all states on the Internet, and court decisions can be researched through LexisNexis. If the assignment had also asked you to research

North Dakota's recidivism rates, however, you would need to explain that multiple studies have been conducted to research this issue and they provide varying statistics. In the body of the paper, you would go into more detail as to why that is true.

• *Establishing the writer's persona.* The introduction lets the writer establish for the reader what sort of person is writing this essay. In this, and in most assignments, the introduction establishes the writer as a professional-in-training and as one attuned to the goals of the course. That is, the introduction establishes the writer as objective, thorough, and knowledgeable. Because much of this is achieved through diction and sentence structure, it may not be something that an early draft is particularly concerned with doing. However, early drafts may help you notice subjectivity in your argument. If, for instance, sex offenders make you angry or upset, that may show up in your draft introduction. If it does, you should determine to what extent you wish to repress or disguise such manifestations and maintain a level of objectivity in the presentation on your argument.

THE BODY

The body is the main part of the paper, situated after the introduction and before the conclusion. The body is where you fulfill the promise of the introduction. If you are having trouble with any part of the introduction, you might want to begin by writing the body and return to the introduction at the end. Getting started anywhere establishes confidence and momentum. Once you have completed the outline and finished the research, it should not be difficult to begin writing any particular section of the body. You should begin the body with an explanation of the facts of the essay and not the opinion section, which will consist of an analysis of the facts. In this case, it would make sense to write sections II and III before section IV. However, it does not matter in which order you write sections II and III, and you do not need to complete one section before beginning the next section.

THE CONCLUSION

The ending establishes for both reader and writer that the essay has accomplished what it set out to do. It may involve brief—or, if the argument is long or complex, more extensive—summary of what has preceded. If there was a thesis statement, it is revisited and restated. It may be qualified as a result of the preceding discussion. The discussion and thesis are related to the broader context established at the opening. How have you contributed to solving the problem addressed? What else might be done or investigated as a result of what you have discovered? Because both the introduction and conclusion relate your essay to the broader disciplinary dialogue about the subject, the conclusion suggests how it advances that dialogue. The conclusion should also explain any limitations to the study (e.g., no studies have evaluated the efficacy of sexually violent predator laws); suggestions for future research (e.g., future studies on sex offender legislation should be longitudinal and show how they affect sex offenders over a period of time); and the implications of the findings (e.g., because studies show that Megan's Law does not reduce recidivism, legislators must consider whether it is worth spending resources on these laws or whether such limited resources would be better spent with alternative methods of community supervision).

REVISING

The post-drafting stage, often called revising, actually has three distinct processes: *evaluating, rewriting,* and *editing and proofreading.* As with all parts of the writing process, these are recursive. What is rewritten needs to be evaluated once again; editing often leads to rethinking and rewriting.

Evaluating and Rewriting

Evaluation of the draft consists of five key steps. First, evaluate the content of the essay. How well did you achieve the goals you established at the outset? Have you answered the questions thoroughly and accurately? Do you support your arguments with empirical evidence? Is your analysis of the legislation well-reasoned? Second, evaluate the organization of the essay. Is anything missing? Should any of the information be reorganized? Is any of the information provided irrelevant? Do you guide the reader each step of the way through the essay? Third, evaluate your writing. Have you clearly stated your argument? Do your word choice and sentence structure assist or impede clarity and effectiveness? Is your diction appropriate? Fourth, check for unintended plagiarism. Did you write in your own words? If you quoted or paraphrased another source, have you acknowledged the source? The final step should be to check for grammatical and spelling errors, which are fixed during the editing and proofreading stage.

Rewriting is done in conjunction with the evaluation of the essay. In addition to the points mentioned previously, this is the point when you recognize any gaps in the content of the paper and identify what is superfluous. You need to add what is lacking, subtract what is unnecessary or confusing, and rearrange for greater effectiveness. Rewriting need not follow immediately on evaluation. If evaluation triggers more research or extensive rethinking, then your rewriting may happen at a later time.

After you have finished writing the essay, it may be beneficial to construct an after-the-fact outline. The purpose of this outline is to conduct a final assessment of what you have written. Look at each paragraph of the essay and see if you can reduce it to a single sentence. The sentence need not be in the paragraph but may be implicit. Any paragraph that resists reduction to a single sentence may be too complex in terms of the content, or it may be structurally incoherent, with sentences following each other haphazardly. Once each paragraph has been reduced to a sentence, check to see that all the sentences in the paragraph are necessary and that they support the main issue in the paragraph. Also check the ordering of the sentences. Do they rationally relate to your argument, with each idea leading to or supporting the main point of the paragraph? Does each paragraph follow the previous one? If you rearrange paragraphs in order to develop your argument in a more coherent manner, be sure to adjust the transitions so that the essay develops logically for the reader.

Editing and Proofreading

This is the final stage of the writing process. Though the evaluation and rewriting stages have helped you to assess what you have written, there are a few final ways in which you can check the content, spelling, and grammar of the essay.

Proofreading the essay carefully for spelling and grammatical errors is generally the last step in the writing process, though you can take into consideration certain factors throughout the writing process. Most word processing programs can check spelling and flag suspicious words. They are most helpful in catching typographical errors but also catch most spelling mistakes. They cannot, however, identify misspelled words if the resulting word is a real word in the program's dictionary. For instance, if you spell "trial" as "trail," the computer recognizes "trail" as a word and does not flag it. The spellchecker often flags proper nouns and abbreviations as well, even though they are spelled correctly. Spell-checking utilities are very helpful, but because of their limitations it is necessary to proofread the essay carefully and not rely on a computer program to catch your errors.

Grammar checking programs, on the other hand, are often too inflexible and unsophisticated to be very helpful to all but the most grammatically impaired. It is best to personalize your grammar checking function. If you have received feedback on your writing, you should be able to identify common errors that you make. Try to determine when and why you have made grammatical errors in the past and whether you are still prone to make them, and make a point of checking specifically for the types of errors that tend to be problematic for you. There is likely logic to the grammatical errors you make. Because you are becoming responsible for your performance as a writer, you need to attend to your own logic of error; if you figure out when and why you make the errors, you can identify and correct them. Eventually, you will stop making these errors.

Summary

The writing process will be different for each person and for each writing assignment, though there are some generalizable steps in the process. You go into an assignment with some knowledge of the topic and the discipline, as well as a repertoire of reading, thinking, and writing strategies. Upon receiving an assignment question, it is necessary to ascertain what the assignment is seeking. At this point, you begin the writing process by making goals and a plan as to how you can fulfill these goals. You next gather research material, read it, think about how it relates to the assignment, and take notes. At this point you can begin drafting the paper, keeping in mind that several drafts are often required for a well-written document. You must evaluate your drafts, rewrite, edit, and proofread what you have written. This process is recursive, in that you may go through these stages several times before the paper is complete. Following these steps should, however, result in a well-written paper.

Reference

Flower, L. & Hayes, J. R. (1977). Problem solving strategies and the writing process. *College English, 39,* 449–461.

4 | GENERAL **WRITING** SKILLS

Writing in criminal justice classes utilizes the same four basic skills necessary in nearly any class: summary, critical analysis, comparison and contrast, and causal analysis. The purpose of this chapter is to explain how these skills can be applied to criminal justice topics.

SUMMARY

To summarize information is to state in brief the main points of a longer communication. Summary is basic to speaking and writing, academic or otherwise. When you tell one friend what another has said, you do not recount the entire conversation but just the important and interesting parts. What you remember of a text or a speech is likely to include the main points. Books and articles in the social sciences are most often reduced to their key issues for purposes of discussion—one reason why direct quotation is often unnecessary.

Summaries should be objective and accurate. That is, you do not interject your opinion or evaluation into a summary. A summary relates to the reader or listener what the source says and only what it says, not what it may insinuate. Summaries may lead to, or be part of, other processes, such as critical analysis, evaluation, or comparison, or they may be the sole task in an assignment.

Purpose of a Summary

Though all summaries should be objective, accurate synopses of a source, not all summaries will be alike. The longer or more complex the sources are, the more summaries are likely to differ. Summaries are done for different purposes in different contexts and these different purposes and contexts will affect the summary. A personal summary, such as a day's entry in a journal, may answer to your private needs or interests: it is likely to be relatively short and highly selective. Despite the fact that you are not answerable to others for personal notes and journal entries, it is important to keep even these summaries accurate and objective, thereby allowing you to distinguish facts from emotion.

Rather than personal summaries, this chapter focuses on summaries for criminal justice courses. They serve the needs of the course, either explicitly in written assignments or implicitly as part of reading for the course. The course provides a context for what information is most important in a source; this key information may differ from course to course, even with the same source. Take, for example, the book *Against Our Will* by Susan Brownmiller (Simon and Schuster, 1975). If you are required to write a summary of this book for a Sex

Crimes course, the key issues would relate to the development of society's understanding of sexual behavior. Alternatively, a summary of this book for a Women and Crime course should focus on the role of gender in the understanding of sexual behavior. The summary of this book in a Victimology class would differ yet again, this time focusing on the changing attitudes towards victims of sexual assault.

This last point needs emphasizing, as many students have had to summarize information only while writing high school book reports. The purpose of a high school book report was often to prove that the student had read the book. If the book was a novel, the student would do a plot summary, describing all the major characters. A plot summary would prove that one had not merely started the book but finished it. In college, professors expect the students to do more than simply read the book (though this is a basic necessity). The college summary of a book or article should also address the following questions: What does the book have to say about a topic related to the course? How useful is the book in adding to the disciplinary dialogue of which the course is a part and in which the student is learning to participate? In a college book review, the student is expected to make the material of the book his or her own. The high school technique of the "information dump," in which one simply picks up material from a book and dumps it into one's book report, will ordinarily earn, at best, a mediocre grade in a college course.

Contents of a Summary

What goes into a summary depends partly on its purpose and partly on its length. A one-sentence summary contains the single most important thing the source has to say: its thesis. But most summaries are meant to be longer than a sentence, and they ordinarily contain:

- The question or problem the source is addressing
- The response or answer the source provides
- Some account of the structure or parts of the source and how each part contributes to the whole
- The most compelling evidence or examples to support the source's generalizations

When the source has a standard format—such as the Introduction, Methodology, Results, and Discussion format of the scientific article—the summary will usually borrow some of the structure from the article, touching on each of the sections.

Summaries should be written in your own words, without quotes. Summaries embody your understanding of the source. They should not employ the language of a source without fully understanding what the source is saying. This is especially important if the summary is not freestanding but a preliminary part of a larger assignment, like critical analysis. However, even if the summary exists for its own sake, the professor is expecting you to translate what the source says into your own terms or terms useful for the course context.

Abstracts

An *abstract* is a summary you write of your own article. Papers in the sciences ordinarily begin with abstracts, which tell readers the key issues and findings with the paper that follows. Abstracts are usually a paragraph long. The ones that precede printed articles are usually written after the article and are summaries of the most important points in the article. Writers, though, sometimes write abstracts for themselves of articles they are about to write as part of the planning process for the article. These abstracts are speculative and usually need to be rewritten once the article has in fact been completed.

CRITICAL ANALYSIS

Critical analysis is an assessment of a source based on careful analytical evaluation, and it is an important skill in the social sciences. Summaries may exist without critical analysis, but critical analyses always embody summaries. A summary, however purposive and selective it may be, is simply telling what the source is about. It does not evaluate. A critical analysis evaluates the source. To analyze is to break something down into its parts or its aspects. Many summaries will begin with analysis, but in a "critical analysis" the key word is "critical." In addition to telling what the source says, the student says what it is worth.

When a professor assigns a book review, the student needs to understand what the assignment entails. Some book reviews are merely summaries of the book, albeit from the perspective or context of the course. But most book reviews, particularly those published in periodicals, require the writer to go further, to include a reaction to the book. The student must then determine how much of the book review is meant to be a summary and how much of the book review should consist of the "reaction," or the student's evaluation of the book. Even if the book review is meant to be mostly summary, the summary should contain an evaluation of the facts presented. It is not sufficient to say that the book is interesting without saying why. It is necessary to explain what aspects of the book are interesting. The reaction may be limited to a single well-articulated paragraph, but never to a single sentence. Rather than constitute a single paragraph, evaluation or critical analysis is often the dominant purpose of a book review. Some summary is still entailed—minimal, if the assignment takes the content of the source as "given" or "understood"—but the emphasis is on the critical reaction.

If the book comes from a list suggested by the professor, you can assume that the book has some, possibly considerable, value both in itself and for the course. Professors seldom ask students to read books that are of poor quality or not of use in the course. If you are choosing the book yourself, you should ensure that the book has value to the course and/or topic, that is, is it cited by other authors? Does it contribute to the literature in this field? Even books of high value are not beyond criticism, and even valuable books with significant importance in any field should be subject to critical analysis. An analysis will always involve a balance of what is valuable and well-done and what is less valuable and needs to be done better. In analyzing, or breaking the book into parts or aspects, one will find some better than others.

To better understand the components of critical analysis, consider the book review of *Against Our Will*. A critical analysis of this book should address some of the following questions:

- *Importance of the book.* What does the book contribute to the literature (keeping in mind the subject of the course and the field of literature in question)? If the book is not recent, is it a "classic"? Is it of only historic interest or is the information contained still current? *Against Our Will*, written in 1975, is considered a "classic" and of significant historical importance in regard to changing attitudes towards the victims of sexual assault. However, much has changed and knowledge of this topic has advanced substantially since it was first published.
- *Type of book.* Is the book academic (containing quantitative, qualitative, or ethnographic research) or popular (targeted to nonacademic audiences)? If the book is not academic, does it contain information important to an academic audience? *Against Our*

Will is a former best-seller written by a journalist; however, it is of considerable importance to an academic audience, because it chronicles attitudes of men towards women and their use of rape to humiliate and degrade women since biblical times.

- ***Objectivity versus subjectivity.*** Does the author's stance on an issue, whether the book is academic or not, provide or take value away from the book? Brownmiller is a feminist and presents very important points from a very subjective view. Although she is the first feminist author to fully analyze rape as an act of power rather than sexual desire, in doing so she often overstates her arguments (e.g., she asserts that all men contemplate rape). It is important to understand and analyze this type of subjectivity and its limitations to the overall generalizability of the author's arguments.

- ***Context.*** How does the book fit into the context of the course? How does *Against Our Will* relate to the issues discussed in a Sex Crimes course, a Women and Crime course, or a Victimology course?

These questions, useful as they are, tend to be more useful when reviewing books than academic articles. For books, these questions lead to critical analysis. For articles published in academic journals, it is more common to critique the article's thesis, methodology, or result. This is referred to as critical thinking.

What Is Critical Thinking?

Unlike critical analysis, which may be explicitly requested by the professor, *critical thinking* is not a specific part of a written assignment. Instead, it is a way to think about the material you read or hear in class. Consider what happens when you receive new information or new ideas. On the extreme ends of the spectrum, you may believe everything you read or hear, or you may challenge or reject every idea. Neither of these extremes is desirable, or even necessarily possible, but the concepts of belief and skepticism are tendencies that, in proportion, help the reader to process new material in an efficient and practical way. Believing or dismissing all ideas, however, is a form of intellectual laziness rather than intellectual efficiency.

When taking a college course, most students will accept statements made by both the professor and the textbook(s) assigned in the course, as both are supposedly authorities in that given area. However, responsible professors and textbooks will indicate when they venture into areas of uncertainty, subjectivity, or disagreement with what others in the field have stated. Sometimes, the professor or text simply reports on several positions without taking a side. At other times, the professor or textbook takes a side and comments on what others in the field believe. It is possible that different professors at the college present ideas differently, too. For instance, a Victimology professor and a professor of Research Methods may critique *Against Our Will* very differently. Conflicting sources may come from outside the college as well as from inside. A previous experience or a newspaper article, for example, may be a source of disagreement with positions presented in a classroom. The key is that professors and textbooks should not tell you what to believe, but should allow you to think about the facts presented and evaluate them yourself. This is critically thinking about a topic.

Criminal justice is a relatively new and rapidly growing academic field, with nearly all criminological research conducted in the last century. As a result, much remains to be said. Many scholars in the field disagree about data, interpretation of data, theory, and policies. These disagreements are not only inevitable but desirable if knowledge is to be advanced. Critical thinking is the academic response to the recognition of disagreement. Occasions for critical thinking in a classroom are the students' occasions for joining the academic conversation represented by criminal justice. It is not valuable in advancing knowledge to simply assent to what everyone knows; rather it is more useful to take a reasoned position about a controversial topic and add to the dialogue. Even if your thinking does not add to the existing literature, the mere fact that you have objectively considered the matter and reached a sensible conclusion adds to the weight behind one of the positions. And, you will discover, once you examine one question critically, that you begin to make choices that affect other problems and aspects of the field, thereby affecting both your personal growth and growth in the future of the field.

How to Think Critically

Critical thinking originates with recognition of a disagreement about issues or data. It may arise while you are reflecting upon lecture or reading notes. It may also arise because the professor specifically points out controversial issues in the field. If the professor is the source of the critical thinking opportunity, it is important to understand the basis of the professor's query. The disagreement may be factual, methodological, or ideological. Factually, information may be contradictory, where one statement must be true and any other false (e.g., "Today is (or isn't) Tuesday," where being or not being Tuesday uses up all of the possibilities). Factually, there may also be contrary statements (e.g., "Today is Tuesday" and "Today is Wednesday," where both statements cannot be true, but they can both be false if it is any other day of the week). Most issues in criminal justice, however, are not clearly correct or not.

When critically thinking about research, it is important to think critically about the research methodology employed, as different methods of researching a topic may produce vastly different research results. Take, for instance, the issue of recidivism statistics on robbery. Some researchers may ask whether robbers have a high rate of recidivism. However, what do they mean by recidivism? If a robber commits another robbery, then he or she has clearly recidivated. If the robber commits another violent crime, is he or she a recidivist offender? What if the robber commits a burglary? The definition of recidivism will depend upon how the researcher defines it. Your professor may ask you to think critically about the results of a study, in which case it is important to analyze the methodology.

It is most common for a professor in the field of criminal justice to ask students to think critically about ideological issues. For example, the professor may ask students to write a paper on the constitutionality of the death penalty. You should begin by reading about this topic. In doing so, you will find multiple articles that do and do not support the death penalty. How you decide whether to support it depends upon the types of facts with which you are primarily concerned. You can address this issue based upon the U.S. Supreme Court decision in *Gregg v. Georgia*, 428 U.S. 153 (1976) stating that it is constitutional. Alternatively, you could address issues related to the execution of juveniles, the mentally ill, the mentally disordered, and so forth. Yet another option is to address the unequal application of the death penalty in terms of age, race, gender, and socioeconomic status, or the cruelty of executing a person after spending upwards of 10 years on death row. There are many ideological ways in which this topic may be thought about critically.

When researching an issue, you may find that facts seemingly contradict your personal experiences. For example, suppose that you read that black male motorists are five times more likely to be stopped in New Jersey than white males. Suppose you are a black male who lives in New Jersey and who has never been stopped. Certainly, you know your own experience to be true. Is your experience of not being stopped relevant to racial profiling? On the one hand, it may not be, because the claim is one of statistical probability, and the experience of one person does not change the probability. On the other hand, it is much easier for someone who has been stopped to agree with the existence of racial profiling, and if your experience has been otherwise, you might be skeptically motivated to inspect the claim more closely. Do all black males have an equal chance of being stopped and all white males an equal unlikelihood of being stopped? Might age, the make of the vehicle, or the racial mixture of the local population or police force play a factor? In such a case, it may be beneficial to cite personal experience when supporting or arguing a point.

At other times, you may find that you read about conflicting facts supported by research. For example, you may be asked to write a paper on the deterrent effect of arrest on intimate partner abuse. You read about an experiment in Minneapolis where, of the three police strategies of arrest, separation, and mediation in domestic violence incidents, arrest produced the lowest amount of recidivism (Sherman & Berk, 1984). Subsequently, you read about a replication of the Minneapolis experiment in Dade County, where arrest had a significant deterrent effect on employed spouses but a significant repeat violence effect on unemployed spouses (Pate & Hamilton, 1992). In other words, the second study partly contradicts the first study. What accounts for this disagreement, and on what basis do you form your own opinion or argument?

To begin with, critically think about the methodology of the studies. Are both methodologically sound? In this instance, both of the articles are published in peer-reviewed journals, so there is no reason to doubt their legitimacy, and both are methodologically sound. Next, consider how each author defines "arrest" and "recidivism." Is it the same in both? Are the populations in both studies (Minneapolis and Dade County) similar enough to be compared, taking into consideration factors such as age, race, ethnicity, socioeconomic status, and employment? It is possible that the contradiction in facts in the two articles is only apparent because the researchers have studied different populations or defined the terms differently. If the methodologies are similar and the differences in study results are real, then it is necessary for you to read more literature on this topic to better understand the source of the conflicting study results. You may find that there is no consensus in the literature about this topic, and you can give qualified support to only one study or the other and suggest further questions that need to be answered.

A List of Questions for Critical Analysis

Critical thinking about criminal justice is a vast topic, discussed only superficially in this book. As you begin to practice critically analyzing criminal justice issues, it may be helpful to utilize a list of questions to stimulate critical inquiry. A good example of such a list is in Barbara Walvoord's (1986) *Helping Students Write Well*. Following are some of her questions, adapted to address critical analysis of criminal justice:

- *What key terms is the text using?* Are these terms being defined in the standard way such terms are usually defined in literature in the field? Is the usage clear and consistent? Take, for example, the term "recidivism" discussed earlier. Again, the author may define recidivism as committing any additional crime, committing only another crime of the type originally committed, being charged with a crime, or being convicted of a crime. How the term is defined alters not only the recidivism rate but also even its significance. If recidivism for a robber involves any parole violation, not simply another robbery, the interpretation of its significance would alter.

- ***What assumptions does the author make?*** Are such assumptions correct or current in the field? And, regardless of whether they are current, should you accept them? If racial profiling on the New Jersey Turnpike is based on the assumption that black men driving expensive cars most likely have no other way to afford them than by selling drugs, we may question whether that was ever or is still true.

- ***What are the implications of what is being said and should they be accepted?*** If terrorists are men from the Middle East, should the Transportation Security Administration conduct searches of all men from the Middle East who fit a certain profile rather than conduct random searches of all those who travel on airlines? What are the constitutional implications of such a strategy?

- ***If a causal connection is asserted, is it supported by methodologically sound empirical research?*** Will raising the drinking age decrease teenage drinking or merely ensure that it takes place where there is no responsible supervision?

- ***If an item is placed in a class, is that classification usual in the field, and is it acceptable otherwise?*** Should those concerned with police corruption be concerned with the acceptance of free cups of coffee and doughnuts? Is this type of "grass eater" the same as a "meat eater," or someone who actively seeks out bribes?

- ***Is information generalizable?*** If the problem-solving policing technique known as SARA (for Scanning, Analysis, Response and Assessment) works in Newport News, Virginia, will it work in Camden, New Jersey? Studies with high levels of generalizability are generally more important for generating knowledge in the field than those with limited generalizability.

- ***If a value judgment is being made, are the judgment and the criteria for it explicit?*** For instance, most criminal justice professionals are interested in prosecuting rapists. However, prosecutors may be likely to offer a plea negotiation on a lesser charge in order to ensure conviction, yet victims' advocates may be more concerned about convicting rapists on the original rape charge to ensure a sentence commensurate with the offense.

- ***Are statements adequately proven?*** Is the amount and kind of evidence used to support an assertion acceptable? In the Minneapolis Domestic Violence Experiment, discussed previously, the researchers found a specific result (lower levels of recidivism with arrests); however, should their conclusion alone drive the implementation of criminal justice policies? (Walvoord, 56–57)

These questions should get you started critically thinking about criminal justice issues. Critical analysis begins with *cognitive dissonance,* or the recognition that two beliefs or facts do not necessarily fit together. Sometimes it is possible to resolve this dissonance by having discussions or reading about a topic from multiple sources. At other times, such readings or discussions only raise further questions. In any case, problem recognition and problem solving are the path to learning.

COMPARISON AND CONTRAST

To "compare" means to look for similarities between two things, and "contrast" means to look for differences, though the term "comparison" is often used for both processes. Most commonly, but not always, the two things being compared have more similarities than differences, because they both belong to a larger classification. For instance, it is possible to compare bench trials and jury trials, because they both belong to the class of trials and share most of the elements of what a trial is and does, differing in that a bench trial is heard by a judge and a jury trial by a group of six to twelve laypersons. The interest of the assignment, then, is in the contrast, or the differences between the two types of trials. If the assignment asks when it would be to the defendant's advantage to choose a bench trial over a jury trial, you should consider issues deriving from the differences, such as whether there has been a lot of negative publicity, whether the issues addressed at the trial are so technical that the jury may not be able to understand, or whether the jurors will be unsympathetic to the defense.

Rarely, the two things being compared do not belong to the same class or are more obviously different than similar. A paper with a thesis sentence that "punishments in Singapore are more like those in the United States than one would suppose" is going to set out to prove either that Singapore is more lenient than is thought or that the United States is more punitive than is thought. In either case, one starts with the contrast and then finds similarities inside it, rather than the other way around.

Organization of Comparisons

Though it is possible to use a combination of structures, comparisons usually have either a block structure or a point-by-point structure. A block structure means that one provides information about the first item and then, in roughly the same order and with explicit or implicit comparison, information about the second item. This is the default structure, the one novice writers often utilize and the one seasoned writers often try first. It is easier to write in this block format, because it allows the writer to simply put together information about a single item at a time.

The block structure, however, is a less effective method of comparison than the point-by-point structure. The reader has to wait a considerable period of time before the actual comparison starts and then has to hold the information about the first item in mind, or go back to check it, while the second item is being presented and compared. Instead of putting the comparable material in two long paragraphs, the point-by-point structure addresses a single topic or point of comparison at a time. This point-by-point structure is beneficial in that it allows for the emphasis of each point, particularly those that are controversial and require detailed discussion. It allows for the full development of the point along with specific examples or evidence presented in its own paragraph rather than buried with several other points.

Which structure is more successful depends on what you are trying to do. If you have one overriding point of comparison (e.g., if you are explaining why women commit far fewer crimes than men), then a block comparison may be best. If you have several points to make (e.g., contrasting men and women criminals by age, socializing, and use of force), then the point-by-point method is more effective. You may want to combine the two structures by beginning with a block comparison to address the minor or less controversial topics and then switching to the point-by-point structure when addressing the more significant or controversial issues.

Analogy

Analogy is a special type of comparison. An analogy argues that two things are sufficiently alike and should be treated alike, allowing for the generalization of information about one item to other items. It not only emphasizes similarities, but also minimizes differences. If arresting abusive spouses has a deterrent effect on further spouse abuse in Milwaukee, we reason that it might also have a deterrent effect in New York. Why should one policy be effective in one American city and not another? On the other hand, if a significant proportion of the abusive spouses in Milwaukee are employed and have a stake in the community, and a significant proportion of the abusive spouses in New York are unemployed and have little stake in the community, the two populations may have a significant difference that would prevent the information in Milwaukee from being generalizable to New York, and the analogy would not be effective.

Analogy is particularly important in legal thinking and writing. The principle of precedent or *stare decisis* says that judges must be guided by prior decisions of similar cases either from higher courts in their own state or from the U.S. Supreme Court. Analogous cases have similar rules, issues and facts. Although trivial facts, such as the names of the parties, will differ without affecting the analogy, key facts—those determining the outcome of the case—must be the same. A single differing key fact would be the basis of distinguishing rather than analogizing the precedent case.

The process of analogizing cases is to begin by pointing to the use of identical rules, which generate similar issues. One then lines up the key facts in each case, usually in a point-by-point comparison. If there are no significant differences in facts, then the cases are analogous. If one wishes to distinguish the cases, one points to one or more significant differences in fact. If one wishes to defend the cases as analogous, one argues that distinguishing facts raised by the opposition are either untrue or insignificant.

Take for example a case in which the police stopped a person and frisked him on the street, without a warrant to search him. Is this constitutional, even though the Fourth Amendment states that persons should be free from unreasonable searches and seizures? To consider the constitutionality of this stop, compare it to the case of *Terry v. Ohio*, 392 U.S. 1 (1967). *Terry* addressed the issue of a "stop and frisk," or a pat-down search of the suspect to discover weapons, which is allowed only if the officer has reasonable suspicion that he or she or the public is *in danger of life or limb*. In *Terry*, an officer observed two men who were casing a store, followed them, and then when they talked to another man decided to frisk them for weapons. His right to frisk based on that suspicion was upheld in the Supreme Court, because he had been a police officer for 39 years and his experience led him to investigate further. When analogizing a case to this one, consider these key points: the basis for the stop and frisk (was it reasonable suspicion?) and the type of search (was it a pat-down on the outside of the clothes for weapons only?). The facts of the cases may differ, but as long as these key points are similar, the cases are analogous.

CAUSAL ANALYSIS

In criminal justice writing, it is common to consider the causes (conditions that are responsible for an action or result) and effects (consequences brought about by a cause or agent) of actions. The discussion of causes and effects shows up not only in free-standing causal analysis but in many other types of writing. Discussions of causation vary depending on whether the topic is scientific phenomena, including issues explainable by physics, chemistry, or geology; social phenomena, including those explained by sociology or psychology; or legal phenomena, including issues related to crimes or torts. Because causal analysis shows up in so many different contexts, it is necessary to develop flexibility in how and why to conduct a causal analysis.

Consider some of the ways in which people consider causes and effects:

- *Prediction.* What might be the effect of something new? Would lowering the drinking age lead to an increase, decrease, or no change in teenage drinking habits?
- *Prevention.* Is it possible to eliminate a cause, or block or mitigate its effects? How do we stop or lessen gang violence in prisons?
- *Improvement.* Is it possible to add a cause or eliminate an impediment to progress? How can we further safeguard the rights of the accused?
- *Explanation.* Link cause and effect. What is the effect of alcohol use on violent crime? What leads to police corruption?
- *Blame.* Establish causation to assign responsibility, establish human agency. Was A's attempted robbery responsible for B's heart attack?
- *Excuse.* Establish alternate causation to mitigate responsibility. Is there a genetic predisposition to rape?

Clearly, causal analysis is not a single unvarying operation. However, note that there is overlap in the following terms and that most are applicable in specialized situations. A *proximate* cause is something happening right before, or near to, the effect. Proximate causes are usually easier to recognize and more important that distant causes. When, in a court of law, responsibility is assigned for a crime or wrong, proximate causes are sought. People who have a last clear chance to avert a situation, as in the driver who might have avoided an accident by stopping at a yellow light, will be blamed for the effects of that specific behavior. A distant cause, for example, that rape may once have been favored as a way of propagating one's genes, is not an acceptable excuse for an opportunistic rapist's failure to curb his instincts.

When discussing proximate causes, it is important to not mistake chronology for causation. Merely because something happens close in time to an event does not make it the cause of that event. Because a rapist watched a pornographic movie prior to committing rape does not mean that pornography causes rape. If many rapists utilize pornography, it may be possible to say there is a correlation between pornography and rape even without the establishment of causality. A preexisting condition or impulse may account for both the watching of pornography and the rape. Or the causal direction could be the other way around: the rapist may be watching the pornography as part of the preparation for rape.

A *necessary cause* is one without which the effect cannot occur. If a police culture that condones accepting favors is necessary for the spread of police corruption, changing that culture will lessen corruption. A *sufficient cause* is one that, often in the presence of necessary causes, makes the effect occur. To eliminate the sufficient cause is to block the effect. If it is the illegality of cocaine that makes its sale such a profitable crime that it leads to an epidemic of homicide, legalizing the drug may cut down on homicides.

As a general consideration of necessary and sufficient causes, it is important to take into account a sense of proportion. Although it is not out of the question for small causes to have large effects, it is less likely that they will. Though the failure to pay sufficient attention to a single FBI agent's report may have contributed to the agency's failure to prevent the 9/11 bombings, most people would look for more significant causes that led to the terrorist attacks.

Because the study of criminal justice is essentially concerned with results for the criminal justice system, considerations of causation are central to most research and discussion.

Summary

This chapter addresses the four basic writing skills necessary when writing in criminal justice classes. Summaries are accurate, objective synopses of the most important points from a longer communication. Critical analysis is the assessment of information based on careful analytical evaluation. Comparison and contrast mean to look for similarities and differences between things. Causal analysis is to understand why and how one consequence may result from another. Effective writing often calls for the application of all four writing techniques in classes and for research assignments.

References

Pate, A. M. & Hamilton, E. E. (1992). Formal and informal deterrents to domestic violence: The Dade County spouse assault experiment. *American Sociological Review, 57,* 691–697.

Sherman, L. W. & Berk, R. A. (1984). Specific deterrent effects of arrest for domestic assault. *American Sociological Review, 49,* 261–272.

Walvoord, B. (1986). *Helping students write well: A guide for teachers in all disciplines* (2nd ed.). New York: Modern Language Association of America.

Writing for Criminal Justice Courses

5 | WRITING FOR CRIMINAL JUSTICE, POLICE STUDIES, AND CORRECTIONS COURSES

This chapter provides an outline of how to write for criminal justice classes. Criminal justice classes can be general, and go over information about all the components of the criminal justice system, or they can focus on a specific component of the system. The criminal justice system consists of three primary agencies: police, courts, and corrections. Criminal justice courses can focus on all or some of these agencies; they often are policy-oriented in their scope. Some universities only offer general criminal justice courses (e.g., Introduction to Criminal Justice); others offer courses specifically in police studies (e.g., Police Management and Accountability, Community-Oriented Policing, Women in Policing), courts (e.g., Sentencing, International Courts and Tribunals), and corrections (e.g., Rehabilitation of the Offender, Correctional Ethics, Prisoner Reentry and Reintegration). Some universities also distinguish classes in juvenile justice into a unique category (the juvenile justice system is separate from the criminal justice system, focusing on delinquent youths and victimization of youths).

The criminal justice system is composed of a decision network, or a series of decisions that turns free citizens into suspects, suspects into defendants, defendants into offenders, and offenders into probationers or inmates and then parolees. There are many steps in the process and each step consists of multiple decisions by individuals and agencies. The first agency involved is the police. The police are in charge of the investigation, arrest, and booking of suspects. The criminal justice system begins when the police investigate a crime. They can conduct a number of activities throughout the investigation, such as interrogating suspects, conducting searches, and so forth. They may begin an investigation because they saw a crime, a crime was reported, or evidence indicates that a crime took place. Once they identify a perpetrator, they must make an arrest decision. After the arrest, the perpetrator (who is now a suspect) is taken into custody and booked. Booking consists of bringing the suspect into the station and registering that the person has been arrested by taking a photograph, fingerprints, and basic demographic information. In addition to actions that specifically relate to law enforcement activities (e.g., ticketing a motorist, finding a burglar, solving a murder), the police are responsible for a number of order maintenance activities (e.g., traffic patrol, controlling crowds at parades).

At the point when the police have arrested and booked the suspect, the case goes to the jurisdiction of the courts. The first step in the adjudication process is the initial appearance before a magistrate, or judicial officer. At this stage, the magistrate makes a pretrial release decision, or determines whether the suspect should remain in custody, be released on bail, or released on his or her own recognizance (or ROR, which means to release a person without bail when he or she promises to return to court for the trial). The next stage in the adjudication process is charging. At this stage, the district attorney (prosecutor) decides whether to charge the suspect with a crime. The formal charge can be brought against the suspect (now a defendant) either by a grand jury (who would issue an indictment) or a judge (who would issue information). Once charged, the defendant is brought before the court for arraignment. During the arraignment, the formal charges are read and the defendant must make a plea of either guilty, not guilty, *nolo contendere* (no contest), or, in some cases, not guilty by reason of insanity. If the defendant pleads guilty or no contest, the judge will then make a sentencing decision. If defendant pleads not guilty, time is set for trial and defendant either goes to jail (pretrial detention) or is released on recognizance or on bail while awaiting trial. Prior to the trial, the attorneys can file a number of pretrial motions (e.g., motion for discovery, motion to change the venue of the trial, motion to exclude evidence). At trial, the defendant may be acquitted (found not guilty) and released or convicted (found guilty, and now called an offender). If guilty, the judge would then sentence the offender to one of many possible outcomes, such as community corrections (e.g., probation, fine, community service), incarceration in jail (for a misdemeanor), or incarceration in prison (for a felony). The legislature sets sentencing guidelines, and, depending upon the jurisdiction, judges can sentence an offender to either a maximum number of years (a determinate sentence) or a range of years (an indeterminate sentence).

Once sentenced, the offender is under the care of correctional services. With a community sentence, the most common of which is probation, the offender serves all or part of the sentence in the community and will generally report to a field agent (such as a probation officer). While on probation, the offender must abide by rules set by the court (for instance, curfew, avoiding excessive drinking, not associating with known criminals). If the offender violates the conditions, probation is revoked and the offender can be incarcerated. If the offender is sentenced to prison (and is now an inmate), there is a minimum time that needs to be served before the offender can be released. Prisoners can be released in one of three ways: parole, completion of their maximum sentences, or upon completion of the maximum sentence minus "good behavior." Once the entire sentence is completed, offenders are discharged but retain their criminal record.

SAMPLE WRITING ASSIGNMENTS FOR GENERAL CRIMINAL JUSTICE COURSES

Assignments related to the criminal justice system are often policy-based, relating to actors in the system, what is legal or constitutional, or what can make the system more efficient. They may focus on the system as a whole or on a single component of the system. For instance, in an Introduction to Criminal Justice class, the professor may ask students to write one paper on policing and one on corrections. Alternatively, the assignment may require students to understand the decision network of the criminal justice system and the link between all the organizations. Consider the following assignment:

> Explain how discretion is used by: (1) the police, (2) prosecutors, and (3) judges. Explain the benefits and problems with the use of discretion in the criminal justice system.

As indicated by the division of the assignment into two sentences, it has two parts. The first is factual. It asks what "discretion" means and how it is employed by three distinct sets of actors: the police, the prosecutors, and the judges. Note that the sets are ordered to reflect the process of the criminal justice system, in that the police initiate a person's involvement with the system, the prosecutor then determines whether to charge the suspect, and the judge determines the outcome of that involvement. The second part of the assignment—as often is the case in criminal justice courses—concerns policy. It asks about benefits and problems in each agency's employment of discretion and raises questions about how to maximize the benefits and minimize the problems. These two parts, although separate, are related. It is not clear how much weight is given to each part, but it is likely, given the policy concerns of the course, that the second part is meant to get more weight, particularly as it requires critical analysis of the issue.

An introduction to the essay might associate the two parts in terms of an overriding thesis for the essay. For example:

"Discretion" involves the decisions of actors in the criminal justice system of whether and how to involve someone in the system. Although the criminal justice system is based on laws that tell people what they must do and refrain from doing, discretion is built into all stages of the system. Laws must be interpreted to be applied (whether an individual's actions constitute a crime) and judgment must be used (if a crime was committed, whether it is worth the time, money, and effort to respond through formal means). Not every lawbreaker can be arrested and brought through the criminal justice process, and therefore discretion is necessary at every stage of the system. The police must weigh the availability of resources with the gravity of the offense to determine whether it is worth their effort to arrest a lawbreaker, have that lawbreaker go through the judicial process, and receive a correctional sentence for the given behavior. They must determine whether formal action in the criminal justice system would help to prevent and halt the lawbreaker's behavior, or whether they might be able to curb this behavior through other, informal, means. Additionally, the police must determine whether it is fair and just not to arrest a lawbreaker, when the police elsewhere may arrest others for the same offense. Thus, though discretion is necessary, it must not show favoritism or bias. Sensible guidelines for the use of discretion should be established that allow flexibility while discouraging inequity.

Note that the first sentence of the introductory paragraph is the thesis sentence that explains the key concept of the paper. The paragraph then provides a roadmap to the rest of the essay. After this introduction comes the body of the assignment, starting with an explanation of discretion in the first agency: the police. Be mindful that this should lead into the next sections on other agencies:

Discretion most often occurs in the intake part of the criminal justice system, as manifested by the officers on the street. It is these officers who exhibit "individual discretion," as they are the agents most likely to come into contact with law violators and must personally make decisions about whether to act. Police do not ignore such crimes as robbery, but may ignore what are regarded as "minor" offenses (e.g., disturbing the peace) or violations (e.g., speeding). Because the resources of the criminal justice system are limited, police administrators may establish enforcement policies or budget resources to enforce or not enforce certain laws (referred to as "command discretion"). Such decisions are necessary to allow resources to be allocated where they will do the most good. On the individual level, officers may regard certain offenses, such as jaywalking, as meant to be rarely, if ever, enforced.

Discretion not to act is in some instances a positive behavior. So many people jaywalk that the police would have little time for other law enforcement activities if they had to give tickets to even a small percentage of the lawbreakers, and the public would likely consider the police overly authoritarian if large numbers of jaywalkers were suddenly cited for such violations. On the other hand, ignoring jaywalking not only encourages the behavior but suggests that there may be other behaviors that, though also illegal, might also be allowed. Transparency may be the best solution. If an increase in pedestrian fatalities has resulted from jaywalking, the police commissioner may announce an increase in jaywalking fines for the laudable goal of saving lives. A change in the policy of discretion is given a public and arguable rationale.

Here, the first paragraph of the body describes police discretion, and the second comes to terms with its benefits and problems. The following section might begin by being compared and contrasted with the preceding:

At the prosecutorial level, some of the same considerations apply. Prosecution is even more costly and may be even more starved of resources than policing, so there are benefits to the system of nonprosecution. A prosecutor, feeling that disturbing the peace is a minor offense not worthy of using limited resources, may dismiss a lawbreaker's case and not formally charge the person. Additionally, if the prosecutor felt that a lawbreaker was only arrested because of an officer's bias, he or she could correct this bias by not prosecuting. Prosecution, like arrest, may respond to political pressures. For example, the mayor may call on the police to enact a "zero-tolerance policy" on nuisance offenses, such as disturbing the peace. In such a case, the prosecutor would likely move forward with the prosecution even though he or she did not feel it was necessarily warranted.

Not only does the prosecutor have the option not to charge, but if he or she does charge, the prosecutor can determine the type and number of charges. The prosecutor may offer the defendant a plea bargain, gaining the offender a lighter punishment while saving the prosecutor and court time and money. But sometimes the advantage is with the offender, as a prosecutor may choose not to prosecute because the evidence is weak or tainted by police behavior, or because the witnesses are unreliable. In this last case, justice may not be served, but the prosecutor cannot waste resources when conviction is unlikely. In such a case, efficiency is preserved, which is a positive outcome of discretion, but justice is not served, which is negative. For instance, if the police arrest a man who allegedly raped his wife, the prosecutor may not charge the man if there is no evidence to support the rape claim. Though this outcome is tragic for the victim, it is likely a sensible use of resources for the courts.

As the essay next shifts to the third set of agents, the judges, comparisons are available to the police and the prosecutors:

Like the police and prosecutors, judges have a substantial amount of discretion. They can use discretion to make a pretrial release decision (e.g., bail, ROR, or pretrial detention). They also have discretion in sentencing offenders who are found guilty, and they can make the determination as to the length of the sentence and whether the person serves a community sentence or is incarcerated. So great are the consequences of such discretion that states and the federal government have adopted sentencing guidelines, giving judges a range of sentences for particular offenses. Some states have also created mandatory sentences (e.g., two years in prison for using a firearm) in order to further the idea of "just deserts," or fair and equal punishment for all individuals who commit the same criminal acts. As with the police and prosecutors, judges may use discretion properly or they may use it based upon biases. It is a telling result of discretion that the individuals who receive the harshest sentences are young, minority males with a low socioeconomic status. Similarly, young, poor, minority males are the individuals most likely to be stopped and frisked, charged with offenses, and held for pretrial detention. Thus, although discretion can be good, it can also be negative when it unfairly discriminates against a particular group of people.

A conclusion should bind the essay together:

Discretion is inevitable. The police, prosecutors and judges must make decisions about individual cases, and the laws are unable to anticipate aggravating and mitigating circumstance of any particular case. Additionally, the criminal justice system does not have the resources to apprehend and prosecute every offender, or to incapacitate or otherwise supervise offenders to the maximum sentence allowable. However, discretion should not be the result of bias from any agency, and if actions become biased (e.g., the police stop and frisk only minorities), then there must be a reevaluation of discretionary practices. All criminal justice agents should abide by the guidelines that exist so that people committing the same offense are treated in similar fashion. Even when discretion is justified by the marshalling of resources, the justification is that criminal justice agents are using the resources to best serve justice.

Criminal justice writing assignments may also ask about the process of justice. Consider the following assignment:

"Does the criminal justice system more closely follow the crime control model of criminal justice or the due process model?"

Once again, the first steps are to identify what the question is asking of the student and to understand the issues. The assignment requires that students do three things: describe the crime control model of criminal justice, describe the due process model of criminal justice, and analyze the criminal justice system to determine whether it is more closely associated with one or the other of these models. The essay should be written in essay format, and the introduction should state the main issues including a thesis statement (e.g., "Since the 1970s the criminal justice system has closely followed a crime control model of criminal justice, though in the 1960s it was more closely related to the due process model"). The body should describe each model of criminal justice and then provide an analysis of each, applying them to the justice system today.

The body should begin with a description of the crime control and due process models of criminal justice, which were first identified by Herbert Packer (1968) in his book *The

Limits of the Criminal Sanction (though they are often discussed at length in criminal justice textbooks). He notes that the criminal justice system has conflicting goals: that of controlling and preventing crime, and that of supporting the individual rights as outlined in the U.S. Constitution's Bill of Rights. The focus of the crime control model of criminal justice is the power of the state, focusing on punishment, deterrence and incapacitation; protecting the public; swift justice from police and prosecutors; and quantity of arrests (assembly-line justice). Alternatively, the due process model of criminal justice focuses on the causes of crime; rehabilitation; individual rights; controlling the rights of police and prosecutors; and the quality rather than quantity of arrests.

When analyzing which model is more prevalent today, it is also important to understand the influences on the criminal justice system decision network. In this case, it is important to understand that the U.S. Supreme Court has a significant effect upon how the criminal justice system functions, particularly in regard to the constitutional rights of offenders. This is because they decide on cases that address constitutional issues and set guidelines for the actors in the system. In the 1960s, the Supreme Court decided on a number of cases that supported constitutional rights of criminal defendants (e.g., *Miranda v. Arizona, Mapp v. Ohio, Terry v. Ohio,* and *Gideon v. Wainwright,* to name but a few). This was during the "Warren Court" era, with Chief Justice Earl Warren. However, this focus on individual rights began shifting significantly in the 1970s, and by the time William Rehnquist was appointed Chief Justice in 1986 it was firmly rooted in the crime control model. For this assignment, you would be expected to give examples of how the criminal justice system is now more focused on crime control. You could point to the focus on retribution and incapacitation rather than rehabilitation of offenders; increasingly longer and harsher sentences, thus resulting in an increasing prison population; a shift towards trying juveniles in the adult criminal system rather than the juvenile justice system; the abolition of parole for many offenses; and the creation of many specific deterrent laws, such as "three-strikes-and-you're-out" laws.

SAMPLE WRITING ASSIGNMENTS FOR POLICE STUDIES COURSES

Some criminal justice classes will have a policing component and students will be required to write assignments about policing. Additionally, some criminal justice programs offer specific police studies courses. Assignments related to policing can cover a variety of topics. They can relate to:

- Specific police roles (e.g., patrol, investigations)
- The police officers (e.g., the "police personality")
- Police management and leadership decisions
- Recruitment, retention, and training of officers
- Different styles of policing (e.g., community policing)
- Requirements of the job (e.g., legitimate use of coercive force)
- Evaluation of officers (e.g., internal affairs, civilian complaint review boards)
- The law as it relates to the police function (particularly in regard to the Fourth Amendment and the Fifth Amendment)

Writing assignments related to the police could draw upon many of the skills discussed in earlier chapters, particularly critical analysis and comparison and contrast. For instance, an assignment may have the student consider a situation in which multiple police tactics could have been applied, and the student would need to assess the situation and provide a critical analysis of it. Consider this sample assignment from a Police Studies class:

> Police officers were called out to a neighborhood where a man was wielding a baseball bat. Six police officers responded to the scene, and all told him to put down the bat. He was clearly mentally disturbed and seemed to have an unusual amount of strength. Whenever they tried to get near him he tried to hit them with the bat. Once close enough they were able to sting him with a TASER, but that seemed to agitate him more and he charged towards an officer with the bat raised over his head. The police officer shot him. Explain whether the shooting was justified, and why or why not.

As with many criminal justice scenarios, there is no absolutely correct answer to this scenario and there are several factors that should be considered when analyzing the issue. First, what is the topic of the essay? A scenario will present a specific example of a situation and will require the student to understand the underlying issue. In this case, the underlying issue is use of force, and the question being asked is whether the officers had a right to use deadly force. Second, to be able to answer the question of whether deadly force was justified, it is necessary to understand the different types of force that police officers can use (called the "force continuum"). Students in a Police Studies class will understand that police officers are allowed to use the amount of coercive force necessary to control a situation so long as it is "reasonable." Finally, with an understanding that the topic of the essay is police use of force, that officers are justified in the use of force along a continuum so long as it is reasonable, the student must determine whether deadly force was reasonable in this case. This requires application of the rules of force to this situation in order to determine whether deadly force was reasonable.

Because the assignment does not say otherwise, the student should write this essay in traditional essay format: introduction, body, and conclusion. The introduction needs to address the main points of the essay and should include a thesis statement answering the main question (such as "The police were justified in using deadly force against the bat-wielding perpetrator"). The body of the essay should begin with a description about police use of force, including what it is, the different levels of force, and when they are allowed to use it. The remainder of the body should include an analysis about this particular scenario, including an application of the rules of force as they would apply to the bat-wielding person. The conclusion should reiterate the thesis and the main points supporting it.

The most important factor to understand when answering this question is how and when the police can use coercive force. The use of force is central to the role of the police, though there are limits to how much force officers can legitimately use. They must follow the force continuum, or begin with the least amount of force needed and progress to more physical force as the situation calls for it. The force continuum begins with nonphysical (e.g., verbal) force, progresses to tactical force (e.g., holding onto a suspect), less-than-lethal force (e.g., pepper spray, TASER) and finally lethal force (using a firearm). Unless the situation presents an immediate physical threat to life and limb of the officers or other individuals, the police should usually begin with verbal commands. If verbal force does not accomplish the task of controlling the situation, the officer can use tactical or less-than-lethal force. These types of nonlethal force are intended to subdue the suspect so as to avoid harm to the officer or others in the area. If less-than-lethal force does not control the situation and there is imminent danger to life or limb, then officers are allowed to use lethal force, or force with a firearm. Lethal force is the last resort of force for officers, and it generally applies when the officers are confronted by a suspect with a firearm or other weapon.

After beginning the body of this essay with a description of the use of force, the analysis should focus on two questions: first, did the police officers use the appropriate steps in the force continuum, and second, was the bat a lethal weapon that put the officers in danger of life and limb? Considering that the officers used two types of force—verbal command and less-than-lethal force (a TASER)—prior to the using lethal force, it appears that they did appropriately use escalating use of force along the force continuum. The next question is whether the bat could be considered a lethal weapon that put the officers in danger of life and limb. Though a bat is not always a lethal weapon, it can be considered one in certain situations. Consider the facts of the scenario: the man swinging the bat has "an unusual amount of strength"; after being TASERed, he is "agitated"; and he "charged towards an officer with the bat raised over his head." If a person with unusual strength were to hit a person on the head with a baseball bat, the effect could be lethal. He was charging directly towards a police officer, and less-than-lethal force had only agitated him. Thus it appears that in this case, lethal force could be considered appropriate.

This assignment resembles the Law Exam Answer, to be discussed in Chapter 7, in that a hypothetical narrative about the actions of the police officers is to be evaluated by applying a rule, in this case about the force continuum. The parts of the rule are applied and subissues discussed, such as whether the bat might in this case be a lethal weapon. In this assignment, the continuum of force is more of a given and less vulnerable as policy than in other assignments. Still, if the policy, as correctly applied, had resulted in an unnecessary and unwarranted death, the policy might be open to alteration.

Writing assignments in a police studies course may also ask for a critical analysis of a controversial issue related to police. Consider the following sample writing assignment related to police studies:

Is there a police personality? Why or why not?

This question is asking you to examine the psychology of police, particularly in relation to their occupation. Is there such a thing as a police personality, and if so, how does it form? Does it make police officers a homogeneous group? Are these inherited personality traits or ones that are developed over time due to the unique occupation of policing? Second, the question is asking you to support your answer or explain how this personality exists, or why you think it does not. As could be expected based upon a writing topic such as this, the police personality is a controversial concept. As such, the response could either support or refute the existence of a police personality and it will be important to support the assertion of whether it exists.

Because the assignment does not say otherwise, you should write this essay in traditional essay format: introduction, body, conclusion. The introduction needs to address the main points of the essay and should include a thesis statement answering the main question (for instance, "Though many studies in the 1960s and 1970s identified a "police personality," these studies are controversial and unlikely to be applicable to policing today"). The body of the essay should begin with a description of the "police personality," which refers to the core beliefs, values, and traits that are common to police officers. The remainder of the body should include support for the thesis statement, including any evidence gathered through readings, lectures, or research. In particular, this answer should provide a description of psychological theories, educational theories, sociological theories, and organizational theories of the police personality. The conclusion should reiterate the thesis and the main points supporting it.

Because the thesis statement claims that research today does not support the existence of a police personality, the most important factors in answering this question are what the "police personality" is, how researchers in the 1960s and 1970s state that it is formed, and why it may no longer be applicable today. According to Joel Lefkowitz (1975), the police personality is composed of interrelated traits such as authoritarianism, suspiciousness, physical courage, cynicism, conservatism, loyalty, secretiveness, and self-assertiveness. This personality can be further divided into two clusters. The first cluster includes traits of isolation and secrecy, defensiveness and suspiciousness, and cynicism. This cluster feels strong feelings of being misunderstood by "outsiders." Feelings of insecurity develop in response to the feeling of isolation and sense of being different. The uniform and badge alleviate those feelings, as they provide a sense of personal adequacy: the wearer can meet the challenges of being a police officer (Wrightsman, Greene, Nietzel & Fortune, 2002, p. 159). The second cluster includes traits of authoritarianism, status concerns, and violence. Typically, police officers tend to be politically conservative, conventional, very loyal to one another, and concerned with maintaining the status quo. They tend to be authoritarian, but more in regard to respecting the higher authority of the law, the nation and the government they serve (2002, p. 161).

Psychological, educational, sociological, and organizational theories attempt to explain the development of police personality, attitudes, and subculture (Grant & Terry, 2008, p. 223). Psychological theories are based on the premise that core attitudes, values, and beliefs are formed prior to entering the police force. Those who are motivated to become police officers have a preference for order and security, as well as a desire to provide social services. Educational theories note that core attitudes, values, and beliefs are formed during police training and the early years on the job. Sociological theories follow the belief that the attitudes, values, and beliefs reflect the culture of policing and are shaped by the demands of the police work. Organizational theories are based on the premise that attitudes, values, and beliefs are formed as a result of the policing culture and the demands on the police officers.

After the body of the essay describes the police personality and how it is formed, the essay should be tied together by reiterating the main points of why early researchers believed that a police personality existed, and why current studies dispute these claims. The paper should contain a description of the controversy over this topic, noting that even though key researchers in policing supported the idea of a police personality (Goldstein, 1968; Lefkowitz, 1975; Neiderhoffer, 1969; Skolnick, 1966), additional research paints a different picture of the personality of police officers (Worden, 1995). Although they do not tend to possess extremes of a personality, most people who become police officers are "normal" or "healthy" in their overall adjustment.

SAMPLE WRITING ASSIGNMENTS FOR COURTS COURSES

Writing assignments in courts courses may focus on the policies or on the theoretical underpinnings of the legal system. They often relate to actors in the system, what is legal or constitutional, or what can make the system more efficient. However, prior to the examination of a system, the goals of that particular system must be clearly established. Consider the following assignment:

> Compare and contrast the four goals of the criminal justice system. Which do you think would be the most important today and why?

This assignment is also divided into two parts, as indicated by the two sentences. The first sentence in this assignment is also factual and asks what the four goals of the criminal justice system are and for the student to explain the similarities and differences between these goals. The second part of the assignment asks the student to identify the most effective goal based upon their understanding of the goals and support why they feel it would be the most effective. This will require the student to draw upon information from lectures, class discussions, readings, and research to support their belief of one goal's superiority over the other goals. Again, the two parts of the questions are separate but related, and it is not clear how much weight is given to each part. It is once again likely that the second part is meant to receive more weight, as it also requires critical analysis of the issue.

The introduction to the essay will outline the importance of establishing goals in a system prior to evaluating its efficacy. It will conclude by identifying all four goals and which goal is perceived as the most effective. For example:

"Criminal justice is intended to link practice with broader social goals" (Brown, Esbensen, & Geis, 1998, p. 47). These goals are associated with certain values and assumptions; some are more sensitive to societal interests, and others are more sensitive to individual needs. Generally speaking, criminal justice theory recognizes four formal goals: deterrence, incapacitation, rehabilitation, and retribution. The popularity of each goal will fluctuate according to social priorities; in the 1970s, for instance, rehabilitation was the most important goal of the criminal justice system and many correctional policies were based upon this goal. However, incapacitation seems to be the most important goal of the system today.

Following this introduction should be the body of the assignment, starting with an explanation of each goal of the criminal justice system:

Ultimately, the main goal of the criminal justice system is crime prevention. Through the establishment of criminal justice policies, one goal of the criminal justice system is deterrence. Deterrence is the prevention of crime through fear of punishment in potential offenders. This goal is sensitive to individual needs by focusing on a potential offender and methods to increase the risks of offending and that individual's fear of punishment. There are two types of deterrence: general deterrence and specific, or individual, deterrence. Policies that aim to prohibit all individuals from committing a particular offense act as general deterrents. Harsh sentences, such as long periods of incarceration for selling drugs, were enacted with the goal of deterring people from committing these offenses. Specific deterrence is the establishment of policies that keep one lawbreaker from recidivating, or committing multiple offenses. An example of a specific deterrence policy is "three strikes and you're out," whereby an offender will receive a life sentence for committing a third felony even though the sentence generally for that particular crime would not be a life sentence.

A second goal of the criminal justice system is incapacitation. Incapacitation is the prevention of crime through the physical elimination of the capacity for crime. This restraint of offenders, often in prisons or mental hospitals, is meant to protect the community. This goal is also sensitive to individual needs, as it also focuses on individual offenders and how to physically stop them from offending. However, it is also sensitive to societal priorities, as it removes unproductive members from society (Brown, Esbensen, & Geis, 1998).

A third goal of the criminal justice system is rehabilitation. This is the prevention of additional criminal acts by offenders through eliminating their motives to offend. By altering the motives of specific offenders, this goal is also catering to individual needs. In the 1970s, rehabilitation was a primary rationale in sentencing and prisons adopted many programs to help educate, reform, and rehabilitate offenders. However, several studies were published that claimed rehabilitation does not work, and this goal fell into disfavor.

The fourth goal of the criminal justice system is retribution, or the punishment of offenders. Such punishment is a "deserved" consequence of the offenders' law violations. Punishment is meant to be proportionate to the crime committed, and all offenders who commit such a crime should be punished in the same way ("just deserts"). This goal is sensitive to both societal priorities and individual needs as it punishes the offender and removes the deviant person from society (Brown, Esbensen, & Geis, 1998).

Note the description of the goals initiates a comparison by highlighting the focus on individual and/or societal factors. This initial comparison not only answers part of the question, but allows for a transition into the contrasting elements of the goals of the criminal justice system.

The next paragraph in the body of the essay should consist of a full comparison of the previous goals. For example:

Examining the four goals of the criminal justice system explains how each addresses societal priorities as well as individual needs. It is also clear that one common purpose of these goals is to prevent or eliminate crime in society. These goals focus on both potential and subsequent crimes, as well as establishing consequences for the offender.

The last section of the body of the essay should contrast the four goals of the criminal justice system and discuss which is the primary focus of the system today. There is not necessarily a "correct" answer, which is why the question asks for your opinion. However, it is important to clearly state which goal you believe to be most important and to support this decision. Support for your belief can be in the form of empirical support, in congruence with another researcher, based upon current policy or based upon state legislation and the way it handles offenders. For example:

While the above goals are interrelated and ultimately strive for the same thing—crime prevention— there are explicit differences in regard to the categorizing of offenders and how exactly crime will be prevented. For instance, deterrence focuses on *potential* offenders, whereas the other goals focus on subsequent or future criminal acts. Also, incapacitation and retribution are goals that are punishment-based. In other words, certain, swift and severe punishment is enough to prevent future crimes. Deterrence and rehabilitation are driven by changes in the offender. Removing motivations or increasing the level of fear or risk involved is the method used for preventing crime.

Which goal is perceived to be the most important will vary by time, political and social priorities. Though the United States was driven by rehabilitative goals in the 1970s, many states and the federal government have adopted a "get tough" approach to crime and implemented zero-tolerance policies for certain offenses. As such, retribution, but more specifically incapacitation, seem to be the leading goals of the criminal justice system today. This is evident through the increase in harsh sentences (e.g., 20-year sentences for drug offenders), mandatory sentences (e.g., an automatic two-year sentence for anyone who uses a firearm in the commission of a crime), mandatory minimum sentences (e.g., drug offenders must serve at least ten years), increase in trying juveniles as adults, and a move towards selective incapacitation of certain types of offenders (e.g., civil commitment of sex offenders at the completion of their criminal sentences).

Finally, a conclusion should bind the entire essay together:

The goals of the criminal justice system are clear. They are intended to link practice with broader social goals through both individual needs and societal priorities. Through deterrence, incapacitation, rehabilitation, and retribution, the criminal justice system seeks to reduce if not eliminate crime. And though the popularity of each goal will fluctuate over time and based upon societal needs, the overall goal of crime prevention remains constant with policy legislation assisting it along the way.

SAMPLE WRITING ASSIGNMENT FOR CORRECTIONS COURSES

Questions related to the correctional system are similar to those in police studies classes. Consider the following example from a Corrections course:

> As a result of "Megan's Law," convicted sex offenders living in the community are required to register their home addresses with the police and the community is notified about their whereabouts. Explain (a) whether this violates the rights of sex offenders, and (b) how this affects their reintegration into the community.

The first thing to do is break down the question and figure out exactly what information is sought. The topic is Megan's Law, the registration and community notification statute for sex offenders. The question raises two issues: individual (thus, constitutional) rights of sex offenders and reintegration of sex offenders in the community. The question is fairly complex, in that it requires the student to understand Megan's Law to the extent that constitutional issues arise from its application and to discuss the effects of the law on the offender's reintegration into the community.

The introduction should address the main points of the essay, including a thesis statement (e.g., "Though constitutional, Megan's Law regulations often impede the reintegration of sex offenders in the community"). The body needs to begin with a description of Megan's Law, followed by an analysis of the issues related to constitutionality of the law and reintegration of offenders. Megan's Law is named after seven-year-old Megan Kanka, who was raped and killed by a recidivist pedophile living across the street from her in suburban New Jersey. The perpetrator of this act was a twice-convicted sex offender who had lured Megan into his house with his puppy, where he raped and killed her. Her parents claimed that the community should know if serious sexual offenders are living in the neighborhood in order to protect their children. Under Megan's Law, sex offenders are designated into a risk level (high, medium, or low) and they have to register with the police for 10 years to life (depending on the jurisdiction and the level of offender). This is civil legislation, and sex offenders are required to comply with this in addition to the criminal sanctions they receive.

Sex offenders have argued that Megan's Law is unconstitutional, because it creates double jeopardy (punishing someone twice for the same crime); it violates the *ex post facto* regulations (it was applied to many sex offenders who committed sex offenses prior to the law being passed); it violates the Bill of Attainder clause (by inflicting punishment upon members of a group without judicial process); and it is cruel and unusual punishment (because it is excessive). Though the courts have required that states implement guidelines ensuring due process for sex offenders in the registration process, they have said that Megan's Law is constitutional, because it is not punishment. To support the argument that this is constitutional, it would be beneficial to include landmark cases that established the constitutionality of the legislation. However, you could also make an argument that cases are continually coming before the courts raising new issues (e.g., whether it is constitutional to restrict where sex offenders live) and the courts may eventually rule that these issues are not constitutional.

In regard to reintegration, it is important to understand how the sex offender adapts in the community. Assigning a negative label to a person (an offender looking for a job must disclose that he or she is a felon) may stigmatize that person and alienate him or her from the community. Doing so may lead to more offenses rather than fewer. In order to determine whether reintegration is successful, it is necessary to address whether the act of labeling the individual as a sex offender and notifying the community about the whereabouts of the offender may actually lead to secondary deviance (behavior that comes after the person has developed a self image as deviant, thus allowing delinquency to become part of the identity). Overall, successful reintegration will be difficult once the offender is labeled. In your conclusion, it would be necessary for you to assess whether community protection sought by Megan's Law is worth the potential secondary deviance that results from being labeled.

Summary

Writing for courses related to the criminal justice system normally centers around questions of policy. These policies can relate to the police, the courts, or the correctional system. Students begin with looking at what is often a factual description of how agents or an institution work and then consider the policy implications behind what they have described and whether the policy might be improved. Whatever the topic of the writing assignment, it is likely to require students to understand the core competencies of writing: summary, comparison, and contrast; critical analysis and causal analysis; and the interrelated decision network of the criminal justice system.

References

Brown, S. E., Esbensen, F., & Geis, G. (1998). *Criminology: Explaining crime and its context.* Cincinnati, OH: Anderson Publishing.

Goldstein, H. (1968). Police response to urban crisis. *Public Administration Review, 28,* 417–418.

Grant, H. & Terry, K. J. (2008). *An introduction to law enforcement and criminal justice in the 21st century: From patterns and causes to strategy* (2nd ed.). Boston, MA: Allyn and Bacon.

Lefkowitz, J. (1975). Psychological attributes of policemen: A review of research and opinion. *Journal of Social Issues, 31,* 3–26.

Neiderhoffer, A. (1969). *Behind the shield.* Garden City, NY: Doubleday.

Packer, H. (1968). *The limits of the criminal sanction.* Stanford, CA: Stanford University Press.

Skolnick, J. H. (1966). *Justice without trial.* New York: John Wiley & Sons.

Worden, R. E. (1995). The "causes" of police brutality: Theory and evidence on police use of force. In W. A. Geller & H. Toch (Eds.), *And justice for all* (pp. 31–60). Washington, DC: Police Executive Research Forum.

Wrightsman, L. S., Greene, E., Nietzel, M. T., & Fortune, W. H. (2002). *Psychology and the legal system* (5th ed.). Belmont, CA: Wadsworth.

6 WRITING IN CRIMINOLOGY AND VICTIMOLOGY COURSES

Criminology and victimology make up a distinctive cluster of courses that contributes to the diverse approaches of criminal justice. More so than criminal justice, police science, courts, and corrections courses, courses in criminology and victimology are theory-driven. Theories are statements explaining the relationship between two or more variables, and they represent general ways of understanding a phenomenon. Theories are abstract, but they generate hypotheses about behavior that can be empirically tested. Criminological theories attempt to explain why individuals or groups of individuals are more or less likely to commit criminal behavior. For instance, social control theory states that the tendency for people to commit deviant acts is controlled by social bonds of attachment, commitment, involvement, and belief. Many criminological theories also explain why certain individuals or groups of individuals are more or less likely to be victimized (constituting a field of victimology).

UNDERSTANDING CRIMINOLOGY

The aim of criminal justice courses is to explain the decision network and policies of criminal justice agencies (the police, courts, and corrections); criminology courses examine potential causes of criminal behavior. There is no single theory that can explain criminal behavior or victimization. Theories can be categorized in different ways, depending on their orientation and framework. The most common classification systems are:

- *Micro- vs. macro-level theories.* Macro theories explain crime across groups or societies and try to answer the question of why there are variations in group rates of crime. Micro theories focus on individuals or small groups of offenders and try to answer the question of why some individuals are more likely than others to commit crime.
- *Classical vs. positivist theories.* Classical theories constitute a school of thought based upon the notion of free will. According to the classical school, individuals commit crimes because of a rational choice, in which they weigh the consequences of their actions and can be deterred from criminal behavior if the costs outweigh the benefits of criminal action. Alternatively, positivist theories are based upon the notion that people are compelled to commit crimes because of underlying factors that can be individual in nature (biological or psychological) or societal (sociological). These theories follow the

premise that people do not make the choice to commit crimes, and crime can be reduced through treatment or reform.

Theories can be broad or narrow in scope, but all theories must fit specific criteria. They must:

- Be logical (internally consistent, not contradictory)
- Be testable (able to be subjected to scientific research so that the theory is verifiable or falsifiable)
- Not be tautological (have circular reasoning)

No single criminological theory can adequately explain all criminal behavior. Theories have developed significantly over the last century, with foci that continue to evolve. The classical school of criminology emerged in the eighteenth century and was led by philosophers, most notably Cesare Beccaria. Beccaria, considered to be the founding father of the classical school of criminology, wrote the book *On Crimes and Punishments* (1764), in which he analyzed laws and called for legal reform. He said the laws were barbaric and arbitrarily applied, and as such they were not deterring people from committing crime. He called for a utilitarian justice system, emphasizing that punishment should be proportionate to the crime committed and it should be swiftly and certainly applied. Classical theories assume that individuals make choices out of free will, and that individuals will be deterred from committing delinquent acts if the corresponding punishment is such that the pain from it outweighs the pleasure gained from the criminal act. The criminal justice system continues to rely on this classical perspective today.

By the early nineteenth century, scientists began to look at criminal behavior from a scientific perspective. Cesare Lombroso, an Italian scientist, was one of the first researchers to empirically study criminals and became known as "the father of modern criminology." He developed the theory of *atavism,* saying that criminals are throwbacks to a primitive stage of development. He said that criminals were physiologically different than noncriminals, and that they were characterized by animalistic, amoral behavior. He believed they could not help but commit offences; rather than commit crime out of free will, their behavior was innate. Thus, positivist criminology emerged. Several other researchers also studied criminal behavior from a biological perspective at this time, such as Gall (who studied *phrenology,* or the shape of the skull and the likelihood that criminals could be determined by the number of lumps on the head) and Sheldon (who studied somatotyping, or the likelihood that people with certain body types are more likely to commit crimes). These early biological theories have largely been rejected today but are historically important in the discipline. Modern biological theories surmise that behavior is the product of complex interactions between genetics and the environment. Most modern biological theories are based upon explanations of heredity (based on genetics), biochemical deficiencies (linking violent or disruptive behavior to chemical abnormalities in the brain that may be genetic or the result of poor eating habits, vitamin deficiencies, low blood sugar, etc.), poorly developed autonomic nervous system functions (thus, resulting in poor avoidance conditioning and an inability to learn law-abiding behavior), or low IQ.

While biological theories of criminal behavior were developing, so were psychological theories. The main focus of psychological theories is the individual and any differences within the mind of the individual, and psychological theories purport that crime is the result of abnormal mental processes or inappropriately conditioned behavior. Perhaps the best known psychological theories were psychoanalytic in nature, developed by Sigmund Freud. Freud theorized that the id (pleasure principle), the ego (reality principle), and the superego (conscience) are three constructs within the psyche, and that crime occurs when the super-ego is weak and the id is overactive. Many researchers supported the psychoanalytic view throughout the twentieth century, though at the same time other theories also began to develop. The personality has been a significant focus, whether on personality types (e.g., Eysenck's personality dimensions of introversion/extroversion, that address social interactions; neuroses, that address emotional reactions and anxieties; and psychoses, that address aggressions and egocentric impulses) or personality disorders (chronic, pervasive, and inflexible patterns of thinking and behaving that are sufficiently maladaptive to cause disruption in functioning).

In the early part of the twentieth century, sociologists began to focus more of their attention on the issue of criminal behavior, though they were primarily concerned at this time with explaining why youths joined gangs. Led by the researchers in the Chicago School, these sociologists looked at issues related to the environment (Shaw and McKay's theory of social disorganization) and the learning processes (Edwin Sutherland's theory of differential association). The premise of these theories was that the environment in which someone lives has a significant effect on their social structure and their definitions and view of the law. At the same time, researchers elsewhere looked at who in society makes and applies the laws. Radical criminologists such as Karl Marx claimed that certain groups in society have more power than others and those are the groups that make the laws, and as such crime and delinquency are products of the struggle between the classes within society. Some prominent sociological theories include:

- *Strain.* Based on Durkheim's concept of anomie, or normlessness, strain exists when there is disparity between success and goals. Essentially, strain theories are based upon the notion that everyone aspires to high achievement and success, and worth is valued by monetary success. Where there is not equal opportunity for all the people in a given area and yet there is a strong emphasis on material success, strain develops. If people can strike a balance between social structure and culture, they will be law-abiding citizens. If not, they will commit criminal activity.
- *Social learning theory.* Based upon the foundation of Sutherland's differential association, social learning theory follows the premise that criminal behavior is learned; attitudes towards the law and behaviors are dependent upon the definitions given to these behaviors by close friends and family, they develop based upon the rewards and punishments attached to them, and imitation of these behaviors occurs. Similar to operant conditioning, behavior is shaped by positive and negative reinforcements; where positive reinforcements act as rewards for the behavior, negative reinforcements act as punishment for the behavior.
- *Control theories.* The premise of control theories is that people are born self-serving and would naturally commit criminal behavior, but they learn law-abiding behavior. Hirschi's social control theory explains that the tendency for people to commit deviant acts is controlled by social bonds.

In addition to these theories, many researchers subscribe to the fact that no single theory can explain criminal behavior and it is therefore better to use an integrated set of theories to explain behavior. The not only helps to explain why individuals may commit a criminal act, but also the development of behavior over the course of a person's life.

SAMPLE WRITING ASSIGNMENTS FOR CRIMINOLOGY COURSES

A writing assignment in Criminology will likely try to determine how well the student understands criminological theories or how to test the validity of a theory. Consider the following assignment:

> Compare and contrast social learning theory and social control theory. Which best explains gang membership and why?

Despite the seemingly simple nature of this assignment, it is asking the student to do four things: explain social learning theory, explain social control theory, compare and contrast these theories, and explain which is best suited to explain gang membership. The phrase "compare and contrast" implies that these theories have similarities and differences and that an explanation of both should be included in the answer. It is not clear whether one theory or the other best explains gang membership; this may be something covered in the class or in readings, but it is more likely something that you would need to deduce based upon your understanding of the theories. Can one theory support the answer to this question with empirical data while the other cannot? Does one have a more logical theoretical foundation that applies to this question? Does one lead to self-contradiction or unlikely causation? In fact, both theories can explain gang membership and can be supported with empirical data. However, both theories also have weaknesses in the application to gang membership. As such, it will be important to explain the strengths and weaknesses of whichever theory you choose.

Unless the assignment specifically states otherwise, this should be written in standard essay format: introduction, body, and conclusion. The introductory paragraph should have a thesis statement that clearly identifies the answer to the question (e.g., "Though both social learning theories and social control theories can explain gang membership, social learning theory does so most comprehensively"). The body of the assignment should begin with an explanation of each of the theories and continue with an analysis of them. The conclusions should restate the thesis and briefly recount the reason for the conclusion.

The length of the description of the theories will depend upon the length of the writing assignment. The analysis of the issue should always be the longest and most in-depth section of the writing assignment. So, if the writing assignment is five pages, the introduction and the description of the theories should be no more than two pages in length. The next task is to compare and contrast the theories. As explained in Chapter 4, to "compare" means to look for similarities between two things and to "contrast" means to look for differences. Beginning with the comparison, both social learning and social control theories are based on a sociological framework; in other words, they attempt to explain behavior as the result of environmental influences. They are also similar in that they are both "social process" theories. Social process theories are those that explain behavior as learned, or more specifically, those that argue that criminality (or lack thereof) is a function of individual socialization.

Despite these similarities, there are crucial differences between the two theories. Most importantly, social learning theories state that criminal behavior is learned from those with whom you associate the most. Social control theories state that individuals learn how *not* to violate the law, or they learn how to conform to the rules of society. Social control theorists argue that the more involved and committed a person is to conventional activities, the greater the attachment to others (such as family and friends), the less likely that a person is to violate the rules of society. Social learning theory essentially assumes that individuals are born "good" or at least that they are born a blank slate. However, if close friends or family have a negative view of the law and believe that it can be violated, and the associates violate the law with little or no negative consequences, then the person learns to imitate that behavior. Social control theories work from the opposite basic assumption, that individuals are essentially born "bad." As such, they would naturally commit crimes; it is not in their nature to conform to the rules. However, strong social bonds will reduce the likelihood that they would commit criminal acts.

Evaluation of which theory can best explain gang membership requires critical analysis of the theories (see Chapter 4 for more detailed information on critical analysis), and more specifically the differences between the theories. There is no "correct" answer to this question, as both theories have strengths in explaining aspects of gang membership. One way to think about the question is to consider three aspects of gang membership: joining a gang, maintaining a relationship with the gang, and desistance from gang membership. Control theory suggests that weak social bonds, such as absent or dysfunctional parents, lack of commitment to school, or conventional activities, may make it easier for individuals to join gangs. Social learning theory suggests that once an individual becomes a gang member, the individual will learn gang values and behavior from the others. Control theory suggests that all individuals would be at risk to commit criminal behavior were it not for the restraint provided by social bonds. Learning theory suggests that only those who associate with criminals learn such behavior. Those who associate with conventional friends learn conventional behavior.

Both theories offer sufficient explanations about maintaining a relationship with a gang. Learning theory suggests that once delinquent behavior has been learned and gang membership established, people will maintain membership with the gang. Control theory suggests that once social bonds have been weakened, they will stay weak. For instance, lack of interest in school, a conventional activity, perpetuates itself. Undeveloped scholastic habits or poor literacy skills make it difficult to begin investing in education later. Gang membership both compensates for lack of academic success and puts pressure on gang members not to invest in academic achievement.

Nonetheless, many individuals do desist from gang membership. Applying each theory to the discussion of desistance may be the best test for which best answers this question. For example, lifestyle transitions, such as getting married, joining the military, or getting a conventional job, are related to stopping gang membership. These functions are best explained through social control theory, as marriage and children relate to the formation of conventional social bonds and attachments. Also, those who are married and have children often find some type of conventional job and take on conventional responsibilities, such as paying for housing and other bills. As such, social control theory best explains desistance from gang membership and may be the best answer for the question. After thoroughly analyzing these issues, a conclusion paragraph can succinctly summarize the key points.

Now consider the following assignment:

> Analyze the labeling theory and describe ways in which labeling can cause *and* prevent future crimes. Would the role of the parent, according to this theory, be more likely to cause or prevent future criminal acts in their children and why?

This particular assignment is asking three things of the student: explain the labeling theory, explain how it can cause and prevent crime, and determine whether parental influence is more likely to cause or prevent crime in their children according to this theory. The term "analyze" implies examining the theory in great detail and identifying its main components. Similar to the previous assignment, it is not clear as to whether labeling and the role of the parent is more likely to cause or prevent crime, or both, but this may be something that was also covered in class or assigned readings, requiring the students to make a deduction based upon their own understanding of the labeling theory.

Using the standard essay format—introduction, body, and conclusion—the introductory paragraph should include a thesis statement answering the question(s) asked (e.g., "According to the labeling theory, the parental role can both cause and prevent crime depending upon how and which labels are reinforced"). The body of the assignment should explain the labeling theory in detail, including what role the parent can play in each of the components and an analysis of how this can cause or prevent future crimes. The conclusion should restate the thesis and outline the reasoning behind the discussion and conclusions.

Once again, the analysis of the issue should be the longest and most in-depth section of the writing assignment. So, for another five-page assignment, the introduction and analysis of the theory should be no more than two pages. The next task is to explain how labeling can both cause and prevent crime. As learned through readings and lectures, the labeling theory is the placement of a label on an individual after the commission of a deviant act (e.g., "troublemaker," "bad boy," "felon"). The placement and reinforcement of this label can push an individual to commit further crimes as a form of self-fulfilling prophecy. In other words, if society views you in a certain way (according to the label) regardless of your actions, why not just act accordingly?

According to the labeling theory, this label can also prevent future crimes. In opposition to the self-fulfilling prophecy, a negative label after the commission of an initial deviant act can push an individual to work harder to disprove that label, therefore eliminating deviant acts and replacing them with productive societal behavior.

The evaluation of the parents and their role in future crime commission according to this theory requires the critical analysis of this theory, especially any other theories that may support the argument. As with many theoretical essays, there is no "correct" answer, but it is important to explain both options thoroughly. The parental role can *both* cause and prevent future crime.

A child's self-concept is developed through the process of socialization. Labeling theory follows the belief that if you think that other people see you as a person who would engage in delinquent behaviors in certain situations, you will be more likely to actually engage in delinquency. These appraisals by others are particularly important in guiding a child's behavior when they come from significant others, such as parents. Considering this, youths who have engaged in delinquent behavior would be more likely to be labeled by their parents. If the parents' appraisals of children are influenced by structural conditions that reflect disadvantages, such as urban location, minority background, lower-class status, and so on, they are more likely to label their child as delinquent. However, if parental appraisals of children are not influenced by such factors, the opposite would hold true and they would be less likely to be labeled deviant, and ultimately less likely to conform to that label (Cullen & Agnew, 2002). It would then be appropriate to conclude that parental appraisals of youths as deviant or conforming will influence their further delinquency, primarily by influencing youths' reflected appraisals of the self as deviant or conforming. Once all of these points have been thoroughly discussed in the body, conclude the essay with a brief summary paragraph of the argument.

SAMPLE WRITING ASSIGNMENTS FOR VICTIMOLOGY COURSES

Like criminology, many victimology writing assignments will be founded in theory. However, it is likely that victimology assignments will also draw upon policy initiatives, prevalence statistics, or issues related to the criminal justice system. Alternatively, they may draw upon the student's knowledge of restorative justice, or the victim-centered approach to justice aimed at making victims feel "whole" again. Consider the following assignment in a victimology class:

> Explain whether a rapist should be able to represent himself in court, and if so whether he should be able to cross-examine his victim. Take into consideration, (1) the legal rights of the defendant, (2) the effect this may have on the victim, and (3) whose rights should take precedence.

This assignment requires the student to understand several components of the criminal justice system, namely, the law, the courts, and the rights of victims. This assignment might have a different response if it were written in a class on constitutional law. In that case, the emphasis might be on the first of the components—legal rights of the offender. Although the victimology course still requires understanding the benefits of defending oneself in court (for instance, defendants may feel that they will not be well served by legal aid attorneys; they may hope to tell more of their side of the story if they defend themselves) and problems (defendants rarely have the requisite legal knowledge to fully defend themselves), the focus in this course will be on how this affects the victim.

The field of victimology emerged because of concerns that the needs and rights of victims were receiving less attention than those of offenders, and the treatment of rape victims in particular has seen significant improvements over the last three decades. Thus, the emphasis in this assignment will be victim- rather than offender-centered.

The assignment should begin with a thesis that introduces the key issues presented in this scenario, as well as the stance you will take on the issues in the body of the essay:

Despite the increase in rape shield laws over the past three decades, many rape victims continue to feel "revictimized" by various components of the criminal justice process. Of particular concern is the right of the defendant to defend himself in court, thus enabling him to cross-examine the accuser—his victim. Though defendants have the right to self-representation, the court must make concessions for the victim in order to reduce the potentially traumatic effect that this could have. This is not without precedent; child witnesses are often allowed to give testimony for closed-circuit televisions or other such modifications, and the same type of modifications should be made in rape cases. The defendant's rights would still be protected, while the level of revictimization would be dramatically reduced.

The first part of the body of this assignment should present facts of defendants' rights and guidelines for defendants serving as their own counsel. There is considerable precedent for allowing them to do so. In fact, there are some high-profile cases in which the defendant has represented himself and cross-examined his own victims. For example, Colin Ferguson, who was responsible for the Long Island Railroad Massacre in 1993, represented himself at trial. He killed 6 people and injured 19, and he was allowed to cross-examine those victims in his case.

The issue at the core of this assignment, which is addressed in the second part of the question, is whether there should be an exception in rape cases. There has been much concern that victims of rape have been, and may continue to be, revictimized by the criminal justice system. Victims have had to deal with skeptical and unsympathetic questioning that makes them relive the shame and trauma of their ordeal as investigating officers and prosecutors rule out the possibility of consent, which is the chief defense against the charge. Rape has been the area where the phenomenon of "blaming the victim" has been most damaging; victims have been held responsible for wearing provocative clothing, being promiscuous, and engaging in behavior that led to the rape (e.g., drinking, staying out late). Victimology often considers how watching their persecutors be punished helps make victims "whole"; in rape trials, the victim may be punished by having to give testimony and suffer cross-examination with the thought that the rapist may go free if the testimony is ineffective. How can the victim perform well on the stand while facing the very person who caused the trauma? Rather than being made whole, such a circumstance may lead to substantial feelings of revictimization.

The third part of the question requires balancing the concerns of the first two. The defendant has a right to self-defense. The victim has a right to protection, to whatever extent possible, from revictimization. As noted in the introductory paragraph, you can offer examples of parallel situations in which exceptions have been made to the general courtroom rules in order to protect vulnerable victims and/or witnesses. The judge would have the discretion to allow such an exception, and could do so after considering the specific nature of the case. To allow the defendant to cross-examine the victim may give the defense an unfair advantage and the prosecution an unfair handicap. If the judge perceives that this might occur, he or she should support the rights of the victim while ensuring that the defendant is offered a fair trial.

The summary should reiterate the stance on these issues and offer potential solutions to this problem. For instance, you can suggest that the victim testify in front of cameras in another room so as not to come face-to-face with the perpetrator. Alternatively, you may suggest that while the rapist is allowed to defend himself, he is required to work with court-appointed (or otherwise chosen) counsel who will be in charge of cross-examining the witness. In conclusion, as with so many other situations in criminal justice, there are no simple answers here.

Victimology assignments may also draw upon policy initiatives, prevalence statistics, or issues related to the criminal justice system. For example, a victimology assignment may ask:

> Does the criminal justice system treat victims of crime fairly? What can be done to improve crime victims' beliefs that the justice system supports their rights as much or more than the criminal defendants' rights?

Using a victim-centered approach, this assignment requires students to identify and clearly state their position on the treatment of victims in the criminal justice system, and support this position with existing policy or suggestions for future policies. Although there is no "correct" answer to the first part of this question, it is important for students to use policy initiatives to support their position.

The assignment should begin with a thesis statement that clearly states the position you will take on the issues in the body of the essay. For example, you can begin with the following:

> Various researchers have found that victims are often dissatisfied with the criminal justice system (Wrightsman, Greene, Nietzel, & Fortune, 2002, 253). A greater awareness of this dissatisfaction, as well as an increased awareness of the effects of victimization, has led to increased rights and fairness for victims in the last two decades. However, despite these recent advances in victim support, more can be done to support victims throughout the process to make them feel whole again.

This introduction sets up the essay by noting that the criminal justice system is substantially better now at addressing victims' rights than it was a few decades ago, but there are many improvements that can still be made. The body should begin with a brief historical overview of how victims have been treated by the criminal justice system in the past and how victims' rights have developed. For instance, it would be useful to discuss how victims were often treated as if they played a role in the offense (particularly in cases such as rape), how they traditionally have received very little information about the criminal cases, and how the offender-centered retributive justice system rarely devoted resources to the victims to help them feel whole again. After this, the essay should address key issues that make victims dissatisfied today, such as the speed of the criminal justice system and inclusion of the victim in the criminal justice proceedings. Issues such as insufficient punishment for offenders and a lack of concern for the victims' needs are also still a concern. Once these problems and concerns have been stated, it is important to support these assertions with evidence.

Before discussing what steps can be taken in the future to improve victims' perceptions of the criminal justice system, you should discuss what steps have been taken already to improve victims' rights. Examples of such steps include compensating crime victims (usually in the form of restitution), participation by victims in crime proceedings (via victim impact evidence), legislative changes protecting victims' rights (notification of proceedings, heard at crucial stages, notification of the release of an offender, and receiving restitution), and reconciling victims and offenders (also known as restorative justice). Though the other responses to victims' concerns have been effective, restorative justice is the most "popular" with victims, as it provides the most in "return," in their opinion (Wrightsman, et al., 2002). Restorative justice produces offender accountability (taking personal responsibility, facing those they have harmed, and taking steps to repair harm and make amends), competency development (offenders learn empathy, effective communication skills, and conflict resolution skills), and community safety. Community safety allows the victim and community the opportunity to tell the offender how they feel, suggest how the harm should be repaired, the opportunity to ask questions and for the victims and the community to regain a sense of safety by bringing closure to the incident (Wrightsman et al., 2002, 253–257). In the summary paragraph, you should restate your position on whether the system is fair to victims and what the policy focus should be to improve victims' perceptions of the system. For instance, because the body contains information about the effectiveness of restorative justice programs, you can recommend that such programs be implemented throughout the United States.

Summary

Criminology and victimology courses generally focus on theoretical issues in the field of criminal justice, specifically the causes of crime and victimization. Like all criminal justice–related courses, they ultimately focus on the reduction of crime and the protection of victims. In order to reduce the amount of crime that occurs, it is necessary to understand why it occurs. Theories about the etiology and maintenance of criminal behavior attempt to explain such behavior at both the individual and group levels. Some theories explain deviant behavior from the decision-making perspective of the perpetrator (rational choice theories), and others attribute societal (e.g., strain) or individual differences (e.g., personality disorders) to the deviant behavior.

Criminal justice and criminology courses focus on the perpetrators; victimology courses focus on those affected by crimes. Just as it is important to understand why individuals commit crimes, it is also important to understand rates of victimization and the impact of crime on victims, their families, and society. Victimology courses attempt to explain this, as well as examining approaches to making victims feel whole again.

References

Beccaria, C. (2009). *On crimes and punishment.* New Brunswick: Transaction Publishers. (Original work published 1764)

Cullen, F. T. & Agnew, R. (Eds.). (2002). *Criminological theory: Past to present: essential reading.* Cary, NC: Roxbury Publishing.

Wrightsman, L. S., Greene, E., Nietzel, M. T., & Fortune, W. H. (2002). *Psychology and the legal system* (5th ed.). Belmont, CA: Wadsworth.

7 WRITING FOR LEGAL STUDIES COURSES

The aim of this chapter is to show what types of assignments students may be asked to write in undergraduate legal studies courses and to demonstrate methods of writing for sample assignments. Although there are similarities with writing approaches in all criminal justice disciplines, each area has unique nuances that differentiate it from the others. This is particularly true of legal studies courses, which tend to have students complete unique writing assignments. The focus is on legal cases and students are often asked to write case briefs or respond to legal hypothetical narratives (as they would in law school). Even though these types of writing assignments differ from those in other types of criminal justice classes, it is still important to consider the writing issues discussed in the first four chapters, particularly the audience, the persona, and the purpose of the assignment.

Although legal writing is used preeminently in law school, it also appears in undergraduate and graduate courses about criminal justice. In order to study criminal justice, it is necessary to know and understand the laws that govern all aspects of the criminal justice system, from the constitutional rights of suspects to definitions of legal offenses, rules of evidence, and codes of criminal sanctions. Two tools for understanding and applying the law often figure in criminal justice courses where knowledge of law is important: the law exam answer and the case brief. The law exam tests students' understanding of the law by having them answer questions and apply the law to a hypothetical narrative. The case brief is a summary of a court opinion that clarifies what the law means and how it is applied.

WRITING THE LAW EXAM

The "law exam" is a common assignment in legal studies courses, both undergraduate and graduate. It involves a *hypothetical,* or a fictional narrative that is the occasion for raising one or more legal questions or issues. An *issue,* in general, may be defined operationally as a yes/no question that can be the subject of a debate (such as whether abortion should be legal). A *legal issue* is a subset of an issue, and consists of a yes/no question that can be the subject of debate concerning the application of a legal rule to a set of facts or hypothetical (such as whether it is constitutional for the police to use lethal force). The law exam presents a narrative that, implicitly or explicitly, raises legal issues. Sometimes the rules behind the issues are provided; more often, the student is expected to know and/or find them. The goal of the assignment is the demonstration of an understanding of how the rule works or might work and a demonstration of legal reasoning as the rule is applied to the hypothetical. There may or may not be a right answer to the question (there are often better or worse answers), but the point of the assignment is not to get the answer but to demonstrate the process of arriving at it. A law exam answer is like a proof in geometry: it is not worth as much to know that the two angles of an isosceles triangle are equal as it is to prove how it is so.

Before beginning to respond to the law exam, it is useful to employ a device called IRAC, which stands for Issue, Rule, Application, and Conclusion. Although this may not be explicitly requested by the professor, it is an excellent way of establishing priorities in the law exam answer. The hypothetical will contain an issue, and the first step is to identify this issue. The hypothetical may explicitly ask a question, but if not, the student must identify the issue based on the set of facts presented. The next step is to look for a rule. A legal issue always implies the use of a rule, which will be used to make sense of the facts. A rule provides a definition of something (e.g., sexual assault) and the application of the rule (the third step of the IRAC process) involves applying the definition to the hypothetical. The conclusion summarizes the outcome of the law exam answer based upon application of the rule to the issue.

Sample Law Exam Hypothetical

Following is an example of a hypothetical and the method by which to respond to it:

> John went out with friends to a bar one night in New York City and met Melanie, who was there drinking with her friends. They talked all night and stayed out even after their friends left. John bought Melanie drinks, and because she felt intoxicated, she asked John to drive her home. When they arrived at her apartment, John tried to kiss Melanie good night. She told him no and said she was not feeling well and just wanted to go inside. "Come on," he said, "I know you want to kiss me as much as I want to kiss you," whereupon he grabbed her in his arms, caressed her back, and forced her to kiss him. Melanie is now suing him for sexual assault. What result?

To begin the law exam answer, start by thinking through the IRAC process. The end of this hypothetical raises an explicit issue: sexual assault. The question posed is whether Melanie has a case for sexual assault against John. Once you have identified sexual assault as the issue, it is necessary to identify the appropriate rule for the issue. Here, it is necessary to understand the rule for sexual assault in New York City. Penal Code section 130.65 in New York State reads, in part, that a "person is guilty of sexual abuse in the first degree when he or she subjects another person to sexual contact . . . by forcible compulsion." Once you identify the rule, you need to understand it in order to apply this rule to the hypothetical. Based on your analysis of the rule and its application to the hypothetical, you can answer the question: what result?

When analyzing the hypothetical, it is important to break it down into *elements,* or parts. The elements may be uncontroversial, or ones that do not lead to potential disagreements; these are *givens,* or nonissues. As in geometry, a given is a fact for which there is no dispute. In this hypothetical, there are at least two givens that relate to the issue. First, John grabbed and kissed Melanie. These actions were clearly intentional, because John explicitly announced his intent to touch her. Second, Melanie did not want to be touched. Although this could be considered a given based on the fact that she told John she did not want to be touched, it is also a given because she is suing John for touching her.

Elements in the hypothetical also may not be givens, but instead may lead to a disagreement. In such a case, the elements are considered subissues. A *subissue* is a yes/no question that can be the subject of debate concerning whether an element of a rule applies to a set of facts. The outcome of a subissue will determine the outcome of the issue of which it is a part. In this hypothetical, the main issue is whether John committed a sexual assault against Melanie. In order to commit a sexual assault, he must have subjected Melanie to sexual contact by forcible compulsion. In order to understand the issue, it can be broken down into two subissues: did the kiss constitute sexual contact, and if so, was it by forcible compulsion? The New York Penal Code states that "sexual contact" is:

> Any touching of the sexual or other intimate parts of a person not married to the actor for the purpose of gratifying sexual desire of either party. It includes the touching of the actor by the victim, as well as the touching of the victim by the actor, whether directly or through clothing.

"Forcible compulsion" means to compel by either:

   a. use of physical force; or
   b. a threat, express or implied, which places a person in fear of immediate death or physical injury to himself, herself or another person, or in fear that he, she or another person will immediately be kidnapped.

Based on these definitions, there are arguments for and against John's actions constituting sexual contact and also for and against whether the actions were committed by forcible compulsion. In considering arguments for and against both propositions, it is important to identify which facts are relevant in supporting arguments related to the subissue and which are not relevant. For instance, does it matter that Melanie let John buy her drinks? Does it matter that she was under the influence of alcohol? The key is to analyze the issue and support your position with the facts given in the hypothetical. Based on all the facts presented in the hypothetical, the strongest argument seems to be that John did commit sexual assault against Melanie. This is because the caress and kiss were likely "done for the purpose of gratifying the sexual desire" of John, and John grabbed Melanie to kiss her, thus implying "physical force."

The law exam answer does not have a specific format in which it must be written (unless the professor articulates a particular format.) However, it is best to begin with either a thesis statement or a statement of the issue. A thesis statement is a summary of the main point of the exam answer (e.g., "The facts show that John sexually assaulted Melanie"); the issue can either be in the form of a question (e.g., "Did John sexually assault Melanie?") or a statement ("The issue is whether John sexually assaulted Melanie"). The law exam answer does not follow the regular essay format: introduction, body conclusion. After the opening thesis statement or statement of the issue, it is best to proceed onward to the rule. The rule is quoted exactly and placed in quotation marks. Do not paraphrase the rule: legislatures often closely consider every word and to change a word is to change the rule. If the rule requires discussion involving case law, that discussion will occupy the next paragraph(s). If it does not, and there is still room in the opening paragraph, you might go on to mention the givens, allowing a sentence for each, though it is possible to combine givens in a single sentence.

Each given must associate an element of the rule and the relevant facts from the narrative (e.g., "Melanie did not want John to kiss her").

Each subissue will occupy approximately one paragraph, or more, if the arguments are complex. The subissue paragraph begins with a statement of the subissue or the conclusion to the subissue (similarly to the issue). After stating the issue and your argument (e.g., "When John kissed Melanie it constituted sexual contact"), you need to state the opposition argument (e.g., "The Penal Code definition of 'sexual contact' does not explicitly state that a kiss constitutes sexual contact") and respond to it. Eliminating the opposition should establish your own argument; if it does not, it is necessary to then specifically make the argument. There should be a logical order to the subissues. If the subissues are interrelated, the logically prior subissue must come first. In this example, the first subissue to discuss should be whether the kiss and the caress constitute sexual contact. The reason for this is that the definition of sexual assault specifies that the action must constitute sexual contact (subissue #1) by forcible compulsion (subissue #2). If the subissues are logically independent, the subissue with the most compelling argument should come first.

In summary, a hypothetical presents you with a brief set of circumstances, and you need to identify the issue, any subissues, and the rule, and then apply the rule. The question in this hypothetical is, "Did John commit sexual assault against Melanie when he kissed her?" The definition of sexual assault in the specified jurisdiction is that sexual contact by forcible compulsion constitutes sexual assault. Based on this definition, John did commit sexual assault, because the kiss and caress constituted sexual contact and they were committed by forcible compulsion. Melanie stated that she did not want to kiss, and subsequently, she is suing John for sexual assault. Though John may claim that Melanie implicitly consented to the kiss by allowing him to buy her drinks and take her home, Melanie clearly told John that she did not want him to kiss her (sexual contact), and when he grabbed her to do so, his actions constituted a situation of forcible compulsion. Thus, the conclusion is that John has committed sexual assault.

Additional Law Exam Hypothetical

Following is another example of a hypothetical and the method by which to respond to it:

Madeline and Valerie decided to go shopping at a local New York City department store. Valerie decided to try on a bathing suit and a shirt. Madeline simply waited outside the dressing room. When Valerie came out, she didn't have the bathing suit or shirt with her. When Madeline asked her about them, Valerie said, "Oh, I'm wearing them underneath my clothes. I haven't decided whether I want to buy them. Let's go check out the CDs." As the two women exited the dressing room area, a store detective noticed a price tag hanging from underneath Valerie's jacket. The detective decided to follow the two women. He saw Valerie pick up a CD and put it in her purse. Madeline didn't take anything, but she was with Valerie the entire time. The two women then walked toward the exit without picking up any additional merchandise. The detective followed them and stopped them just outside the exit, arresting both women. What result?

Thinking through the IRAC process, the explicit issue for Valerie is larceny. Does the local department store have a case against Valerie? Do they have a case against Madeline? Again, it is necessary to understand the rule, and for this hypothetical the rule is larceny. Because the two girls were arrested outside a New York City department store, penal code section 155.05 in New York State reads that "a person steals property and commits larceny when, with intent to deprive another of property or to appropriate the same to himself or a to a third person, he wrongfully takes, obtains or withholds such property from an owner thereof." The next step is to analyze and apply this rule to the hypothetical.

The analysis will begin by identifying the *elements*. There are at least four *givens* in this hypothetical that relate to the issue. First, Valerie took and hid clothing (merchandise) under her own clothing. Second, Valerie took a CD and placed it into her purse. Third, Valerie left the store without paying for any of the concealed merchandise, and fourth, Madeline did not conceal or take any merchandise, but witnessed Valerie's actions.

This hypothetical also has one *subissue:* Madeline's culpability. If a person intentionally assists another person to engage in conduct that constitutes an offense, that is known as accomplice liability. *State v. Hoselton* (1988) states that defendants are liable as accomplices if they (1) have assisted or encouraged or failed to perform a legal duty to prevent the offense (2) with the *intent* to promote or facilitate the commission of a crime. Based upon this definition, there are arguments for and against whether Madeline can be charged as an accomplice. So which facts are relevant in supporting arguments related to the subissue?

The key is to support your position with the facts given in the hypothetical. Based upon those facts, Valerie is guilty of larceny and Madeline may not be liable as an accomplice. Valerie clearly exited the store without paying for the merchandise she concealed. Concealing the items displays her intent to steal, and leaving the store with those items changes the intent to the commission of a crime. Madeline, however, does not take any merchandise and questions Valerie about her intent to pay for the concealed items. Though she failed to perform a legal duty to prevent the offense, Madeline's lack of prior knowledge of what Valerie intended to do, questioning her actions and not having Valerie take any merchandise "for her" supports a lack of intent to facilitate the commission of a crime.

Recalling that there is no specific format for the law exam answer, it is best to begin with a thesis statement or a statement of the issue. This can be done by summarizing the main point of the answer (e.g., "The facts show Valerie committed larceny but Madeline is not liable as an accomplice") or forming a question (e.g., "Did Valerie commit larceny? Can Madeline be charged as an accomplice?") or stating the issue (e.g., "This issue is whether Valerie committed larceny and Madeline can be charged as her accomplice"). After the opening thesis statement or statement of the issue, the rule is quoted exactly and placed in quotation marks. Any applicable case law discussion will follow. It is important to mention any givens as they apply to any element of the rule. If no case law discussion follows, the givens must still be mentioned (e.g., "Valerie placed a CD into her purse").

Each subissue should occupy approximately one paragraph, and more if the argument is complex. Similarly to the issue, each paragraph will begin with a statement of the subissue and end with a conclusion for the subissue. After stating the issue and your argument (e.g., "When Valerie exited the store it constituted larceny"), you need to state the opposition argument (e.g., "The Penal Code definition of 'larceny' does not explicitly state that concealment constitutes larceny") and respond to it. It is important to specifically state your argument, especially if it is not made clear by eliminating the opposition. The subissues should be in logical order. In this example, the first subissue should involve Valerie's hiding the bathing suit and shirt under her own clothing. The reason for this is that the definition of larceny specifies that the action must (1) intend to deprive another of property (e.g., concealing the merchandise displays her intent to take the items without paying for them) and (2) wrongfully takes, obtains or withholds such property from an owner thereof (e.g., Valerie left the store without paying for the concealed merchandise). As stated in the previous example, the subissue with the most compelling argument will come first if the subissues are logically independent.

To summarize, the question in this hypothetical is, "Did Valerie commit larceny and is Madeline liable as an accomplice?" The definition of larceny in the specified jurisdiction is that intent to deprive another of property by wrongfully taking or obtaining the property from its owner. Based upon this definition, Valerie did commit larceny, because she deprived the New York City department store of its merchandise by concealing it under her clothing and in her purse and leaving the store without paying for the items. Even though she told her friend she was still thinking about the purchase, she left the store without attempting to pay for the items. Madeline cannot be held liable as an accomplice. She did not have the intent to aid in the commission of a criminal act. Thus, the conclusion is that Valerie committed larceny and Madeline is not liable as an accomplice.

WRITING THE CASE BRIEF

A case brief is a report on a court case that has already been decided in a state or federal appeals court or the U.S. Supreme Court. A case brief is different than a trial brief. Trial briefs are addressed to judges and concern procedures or matters at trial and are written on behalf of either the petitioner or the defendant. They are necessarily lengthy in order to advocate a position for the side represented. Alternatively, case briefs are short (about two pages), useful summaries of cases. Unlike many criminal justice assignments, the case brief is not written in essay format. Instead, the case brief is a series of labeled parts, responding to questions about the case.

There is general consensus about what needs to be included in a case brief and the format in which it is written. However, some professors will ask for variations in approach and format and you need to be clear on what information the professor is seeking in the assignment.

Most importantly, cases that are not decided unanimously may include the majority opinion (the decision of the court), concurring opinions (where judges joining the majority wish to express a different rationale for their agreement), and dissenting opinions (statements by the minority justices expressing a rationale for their disagreement). The assignment may clarify when you need to include only the majority opinions or when you also need to include concurring and dissenting opinions. If the purpose of the brief is merely to discover the law, only the majority opinion is briefed, but if the purpose is to study the court's thinking or to predict a direction for the court, the concurring and dissenting opinions may also be included. The case brief is an objective assignment and should not include your personal opinion about the issue.

Unless otherwise specified, case briefs contain the following elements in the order presented here.

Facts

This is a summary of the key facts of the case. Most opinions contain far more facts than are needed to understand the court's reasoning for its decision. *Key facts* are those that are essential to the finding in the case. This section should contain the facts the court relied on in its reasoning, as well as the background information that may help the key facts to make sense. Facts unrelated to issues, holdings, and reasoning should be omitted. Facts related to the case are often clustered in the first third of the court's written opinion. Facts stated more than once or referred to later in the opinion are usually worth including, such as the parties to the case, the point(s) of controversy between them, and the legal history of the case prior to its appearance before the court whose opinion you are briefing. The fact section should be only a paragraph or two in length.

Issues

Legal issues are yes/no questions concerning whether a rule applies to a set of facts, where there is plausible or actual disagreement about the outcome (e.g., whether the three-strikes punishment laws are constitutional under the Eighth Amendment). Appellate courts focus on issue of law rather than fact. Issues of fact (e.g., whether the evidence supports the conviction) are regarded by the appeals court either as resolved or as the basis for remanding the case back to a lower court. Issues of law (such as the constitutionality of a law) are the questions the court must answer to reach its opinion. Many opinions will also contain subissues, which concern the application of an element of the rule rather than the whole rule (for instance, whether the three strikes laws are constitutional with both violent and/or property crimes). It is up to the student to determine which subissues are directly related to the opinion and which are worth including in this section. Although you want to avoid listing unimportant subissues, you need to include enough so that the reasoning section of the case brief will make sense.

Issues are normally stated early in the opinion, often just before or just after the facts, and issues normally structure the argument. There should be an exact congruence between issues and holdings: one issue for each holding. When writing this section of the case brief, it is best to number the issues.

Holdings

The holding is the decision of the court. Holdings are single-sentence answers to the issues, numbered to correspond to the issues. Because an issue is a yes/no question, a holding could be a simple yes or no, but it is preferable to state the holding in a declarative sentence. This way it may have a rule-like appearance that lends it utility and makes it congruent with the reasoning. Holdings in opinions are often stated either just after issue statements or as conclusions to arguments following an issue statement. Holdings are very important and are sometimes repeated for emphasis or grouped together in a summation at the end of the opinion. Holdings may be premises for further argument. The implications of holdings are often discussed, and holdings are often qualified by being explicitly contrasted with what the judges do not intend with the holding.

Disposition

The disposition is the agreement with (affirm) or disagreement with (reverse) the decision of the lower court. For the lawyers and parties to the case, the disposition is the main point of the opinion, because it announces the finding of the court. It is almost always explicitly stated at or near the end of the opinion, and sometimes near the beginning as well.

Reasoning

The reasoning is the explanation for the holding(s) and should provide sufficient justification for the holdings. The court's reasoning for the holding is the most important part of and longest section of the opinion. Consequently, the reasoning should be the longest section of the case brief as well. The reasoning section should focus on the key legal explanations for the holdings and should include the information most useful to understanding the case. Care must be taken not to confuse reference to other people's reasoning (e.g., that of the lower court or of the losing side) from the reasoning the opinion espouses. It is important to link the reasoning to the holdings and the disposition.

There are different ways in which to write the reasoning section of a case brief. One possibility is to number the reasoning sections so that they correspond with to issues and holdings, but that is helpful only if the reasonings for all holdings are distinct. Another and more appropriate way to write this section is as a single, structured argument. If there are multiple issues and holdings, the reasoning does not have to address them all equally.

Rules

A rule is the court's interpretation of a statute, element of the Constitution, or other court finding that helps to interpret an issue. There are two sorts of rules: those that existed prior to the case whose opinion you are reading, and those created as a result of the case. Preexisting rules are generally those in statutes or in the state or the U.S. Constitution. New rules created as a result of the case usually relate to interpretation of statutes or the Constitution. For example, the Fourth Amendment to the U.S. Constitution forbids "unreasonable searches"; this is a preexisting rule. However, the Constitution does not specify what makes a search "reasonable." If the opinion introduces a new understanding of how a search may be considered reasonable as a way of resolving the Fourth Amendment issue raised by the case, that new understanding achieves a rule-like status and should be noted in the "Rule" section. Opinions normally refer to preexisting rules and quote the relevant parts of them early in the opinion. New rules are usually significantly emphasized throughout the court's reasoning. The new rule, when it is created, exists to resolve an issue of interpretation of the preexisting rule and is the basis for resolving the issue.

TIPS FOR WRITING THE CASE BRIEF

Case briefs are a unique type of assignment in the field of criminal justice. Here are some tips that may assist in making the assignment clearer and may make the writing process easier:

- *Make sure to identify the correct case.* If a case has been through multiple appellate processes, there will likely be more than one case with the same title. Generally, the assignment will call for you to write a case brief about the opinion given by the highest court. Also, if the professor provides the case number, you can identify from which court the case has come. When you write the assignment, you will need to begin by writing down the full name, citation, and year of the case.
- *Read the opinion twice.* It is beneficial to read through the opinion twice; first, skim the opinion to get a sense of what the case is about, and then read it in more detail. Many

opinions, especially Supreme Court opinions, are long and may have extensive digressions or long strings of quotations and citations that do little to advance the argument. It is useful to note where these are during your skimming so that you do not need to read them carefully later.

- *Take notes.* Write down the headings listed previously and prepare to take notes as you read through the case. Keep in mind that the most information will come under the facts and reasoning sections of the brief. As these are just notes, there is no one place you must start. Remember that the issue is likely to be stated at the beginning of the opinion. The opinion will probably summarize the legal history of the case near the issue. This legal history will give you the basis for the disposition, because it tells you how the lower court held in this case. The disposition in the given case will likely be at the end of the opinion, though it may be at the beginning as well. Knowing the disposition will help you to understand the case, as the issues must be resolved in such a way as to reach the disposition, the reasoning leads to the disposition, and the key facts are those that lead to the disposition. Sometimes the opinion will explicitly state what you are looking for. A sentence beginning, "The issue is . . ." will contain an issue, and "We hold . . ." will introduce a holding. Be cautious of two things. First, the verb should be in the present tense: past tense indicates legal history (e.g., "the courts have held . . ."). Second, check for congruency. If you are not sure if a sentence beginning, "We hold . . ." has a proper holding, check to see whether there is an issue to which it responds.

- *Use what you know to find what you do not know.* Taking notes on a case is like doing a crossword puzzle. You may begin by trying to solve 1-Across, but if you do not know it, you start with something you can solve. Similarly, in a brief, you start with what is clearly identifiable. Again, congruency is important; everything should fit together. Because an *issue* concerns how a *rule* applies to *facts,* an issue statement will contain words referring to a rule. The prominence of facts should lead you to wonder why they are prominent. Knowing which rule is being applied should lead you to anticipate issues. Because *holdings* answer issue questions, it is easy to turn one into the other, and holdings, just like issues, refer to rules and facts. The *reasoning* is justifying the holdings and leading to the disposition, so the reasoning and holdings are dependent on each other and say the same things, either as conclusion (holding) or as argument (reasoning). The *reasoning* is applying the *rule* and making use of key *facts.* Everything must fit together. If you find something that contradicts something else, regard it with suspicion.

- *Quote sparingly.* It is best if the brief consists of your understanding of what the case says in your own words. There are two good reasons for summarizing the opinion rather than quoting excessively. First, your words are likely to be shorter and clearer than the opinion's and therefore more useful for purposes of summary. Second, and more importantly, the act of translating fosters understanding. An exception concerns *rules.* These should always be quoted, though you may allow yourself an ellipsis (. . .) to omit unimportant parts of the rule or *italic* to emphasize important parts (always acknowledging that you have added the emphasis). Because the language of rules is exact, and often the result of much debate, to paraphrase a rule may be to change it.

- *Do not editorialize.* A case brief is a report that is meant to be neutral. Do not use subjective language that characterizes the reasoning, holding, or issues, even if you disagree with the holding of the court.

SAMPLE CASE BRIEF

The best way in which to understand how to write a case brief is to see an example. The following case, *Nicholson v. Connecticut Half-Way House,* is a civil case from the state of Connecticut (which affects its value as precedent, depending on whether it is to be applied in or out of state). There is one clear issue and two subissues, and the opinion clearly states the holding and the disposition.

Nicholson v. Connecticut Half-Way House, 153 Conn. 507 (1966)

FACTS

Nicholson and other residents of Irving Street in Hartford want an injunction preventing the opening of the Half-Way House, a residence for parolees from the state prison, on their block. The lower court found for Nicholson and declared that the House would be a nuisance. The House would have a small number of parolees, exclude criminals with the highest risk of recidivism, and provide jobs and counseling.

ISSUES

1. Is the House an "equitably abatable nuisance" because it will make unreasonable use of the property?
2. That is, will it cause the crime rate on the block to go up?
3. Will it depreciate the real-estate values?

HOLDINGS

1. "There has been an insufficient factual showing that the defendant will make any unreasonable use of the property. . . ."
2. The residents do not appear likely to commit crimes.
3. The real-estate values are likely to go down, but that is not by itself the basis for establishing a nuisance.

DISPOSITION

Reversed

REASONING

The grounds for issuing an injunction before the House has opened are more rigorous that if it had opened and there were already troublesome behavior. The Plaintiff provides nothing more that subjective fear of crime and a false analogy with a town dump. The court finds the plans for the House to be plausible: it should do its job. Therefore, there is no basis for an injunction.

RULE

There are various possibilities. One is "If the elements of a nuisance are clearly demonstrated, and if irreparable harm cannot otherwise be prevented, the court may enjoin the use objected to."

ADDITIONAL SAMPLE CASE BRIEF

The following case, *New York v. Belton,* is a criminal case from the state of New York (again, which affects its value as precedent, depending on whether it is to be applied in or out of state). There are two clear issues in this case, and the opinion clearly states the holding and the disposition.

New York v. Belton, 453 U.S. 454 (1981)

FACTS

A trooper stopped a speeding vehicle with four men inside. Mr. Belton was driving. The trooper smelled burnt marijuana and saw an envelope marked "Supergold" in the vehicle. He associated the envelope with marijuana. The trooper then told the men to get out of the car and placed them under arrest for possession of marijuana. The four men were then separated. The trooper opened the envelope marked "Supergold" and discovered marijuana. The arrestees were advised of their Miranda rights. The trooper then proceeded to search each individual and then the passenger area of the car. A jacket belonging to Belton was found on the back seat and cocaine was found in the pocket by the trooper. The appellate court ruled that this search was illegal, because the officers did not attain a warrant.

ISSUE

1. Can the "custodial arrest" of an individual occur as a result of a traffic stop?
2. What is the defendant's legal standing in regard to the subsequent search of the vehicle and the contents inside the car?

HOLDINGS:

1. The court held that the policeman had made a lawful custodial arrest of the occupant of an automobile and,
2. As a result of that lawful arrest, he may, as a contemporaneous incident of that arrest, search the passenger compartment of that automobile.

DISPOSITION

Reversed

REASONING

The Appellate division of the New York Supreme Court upheld the constitutionality of the search and seizure even though the officers did not have a warrant. They recognized that the urgent nature of the situation made exemptions from the warrant requirements imperative. Belton extended the "Chimel" rule (based on the case of *Chimel v. California*), providing that searches of the immediate area incident to arrest are lawful not just of residences but also of vehicles.

RULE

The court states that the first principle of Fourth Amendment is that "police may not conduct a search unless they first convince a neutral magistrate that there is probable cause to do so." However, warrantless searches of the immediate area are allowed incident to arrest.

Summary

There are two primary types of assignments in legal studies courses: the law exam answer and the case brief. These assignments are related in that both involve similar thinking processes. In the law exam answer, it is the student who proposes a problem, finds the rules, and reasons through the application of the rules to the relevant facts. In the case brief, a judge has done these tasks. However, the student must be able to recognize the question posed by the judge, the issue(s) raised, and the legal reasoning for the disposition. The ability to locate, organize, and analyze the appropriate legal issues and reasoning is key to both assignments.

SECTION III

Research-Oriented Writing

8 | THE **LITERATURE** REVIEW

Most students in upper-level undergraduate criminal justice classes will have to write a research paper. Graduate students are usually required to conduct their own empirical research and write a thesis or dissertation. Undergraduates, on the other hand, are usually required to write a term paper for some of their classes, perhaps 10 pages in length, and additionally some will write an undergraduate or honors thesis. All of these assignments may require a summary of the information that has been written on a topic area. This summary of the literature, called a *literature review,* is a synthesis of all the relevant articles and books in the topic area of the research. It is an account of the relevant reading you did to enrich your understanding of the field, and the literature review must convey this understanding to the reader. It requires you to understand what is relevant and important, and to summarize this information effectively. The literature review may be an assignment in itself or part of a larger research project. The purpose of this chapter is to explain how to approach and write the literature review (including the sources of literature available), how to analyze the quality of the information, and how to summarize it concisely.

CHOOSING A TOPIC

The type of research that students will conduct varies significantly, because the field of criminal justice is multidisciplinary and incorporates legal, psychological, and sociological components. However, there are commonalities in the writing process for all types of research in the field of criminal justice. The first step to take in any research project is to choose a topic. There are four methods of guidance that a professor can give students in regard to research paper topics:

- The professor gives students a specific topic.
- The professor gives students a choice of specific topics.
- The professor gives a range of issues from which students choose a topic.
- The professor gives students no guidance on the topic.

In some classes, the decision of what to write is made for you, because the professor will give you a specific research topic. For instance, the professor in a "Women in Policing" class may require a term paper on the integration of women into the police force throughout the century. Another possibility is that the professor will give you a choice of topics, narrowly defined. So, instead of giving you one specific topic, the professor of the "Women in Policing" class may ask you to choose from the following topics: the integration of women in the police force throughout the century, the differences between male and female police officers, or a summary of the legislation and police practices that have encouraged more women and minority officers to join the police force in the last 40 years. If the professor gives you a topic or choice of topics, you have a starting point from which to work and the topic will most likely guide you as to how to begin your search for books and articles.

The next possibility is that the professor does not give you specific direction for a topic. The professor may give you a broad area from which to choose a topic, and you need to decide what to research. For example, if you are in a "Criminological Theory" class, the professor may give you the following assignment:

> Explain the development of a theory we have discussed in class, including the theorists associated with it.

This is a very broad question, and it is important for any research assignment that you narrow the scope as much as possible. This question is best approached by breaking theories down into their most basic components. First, what are the different categories and subcategories of theories? Second, who developed these theories? Third, how are the theories related to each other? This question is further complicated when we look at different criminological theories and realize that they can be broken down in several ways. For instance, theories can divided into broad categories of macro-level or micro-level theories, depending upon whether they are assessing differences in crime rates within groups or individuals, respectively. Alternatively, they can be divided broadly into categories of classical or positivist theories, depending upon whether they are based upon the philosophical concept of free will or the scientific viewpoint that criminal behavior results from factors beyond a person's free will and choices. Positivist theories can further be broken down into biological, psychological and sociological/sociocultural theories, all of which can be even further broken down into specific theories.

The best way to go about this assignment would be to begin from the individual theory level. Presumably, in a theory class you have already received lectures and read books on specific theories. This assignment calls for an analysis of the development of a specific theory and the theorists involved. Thus, identify a theory and work up through the classification system. As an example, take routine activities theory, proposed by Cohen and Felson (1979). Routine activities theory states that in order for a crime to occur, there must be a motivated offender, a target, and a lack of a capable guardian. If these three factors exist at any given time and space, then a crime can occur. This is a micro-level theory; it explains why an individual may commit a crime, but it does not explain differences in crime rates amongst groups. It also involves decision making based upon the potential consequences; thus, it would be considered within the field of rational choice theories. Rational choice theories developed from the classical school, following Beccaria and Bentham's philosophy that in order to prevent crime, the laws must be just severe enough to deter potential criminals. They also explained that in order for deterrence to be effective, the punishment must be swift and certain. Following this idea and applying it to situational crime, Clarke (1997) developed the concept of situational crime prevention, proposing that the existence of a capable guardian (e.g., closed-circuit TV, or CCTV) where there is a potential target (such as an ATM) would ensure punishment (it is certain they would be seen), and thus it would deter the motivated offenders from committing crimes (assuming that the punishment for the crime would be severe enough). Though this overview, as charted in Figure 8.1, is brief, it shows the

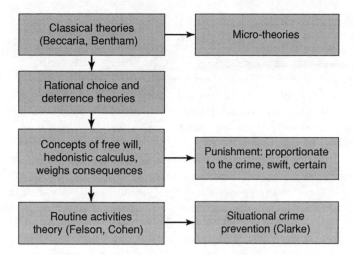

FIGURE 8.1. Conceptual development of routine activities theory.

development of the theory, its classification system, and the theorists involved. The remainder of the term paper would further develop these points.

The final possibility for choosing a topic is that the professor does not offer any topic choices. When the professor gives you no guidance for a topic, which is common in writing a thesis, then you need to decide what, in the entire field of criminal justice, you are most interested in writing about, and what it is possible to write about in the given page limit. When choosing a topic, first consider the broad area of criminal justice that you are interested in studying. Do you want to study issues related to criminological theory, corrections, policing, the juvenile justice system, or the law? What issues within these broad topics interest you? Once you decide upon your broad area of interest, you need to make three more decisions: first, what would you like to study specifically within that broad area; second, is there enough information on this topic that you can summarize; third, is the scope of the project appropriate for your assignment?

Of all the criminal justice topics you have studied, let's assume that you are most intrigued by the topic of corrections. Thus, you decide to conduct research in this area. But what would you like to study within that broad topic area? You can break down corrections first into three subcategories: community corrections, correctional institutions, and prisoner reentry. If you decide to conduct research on a topic related to correctional institutions, you must break this down further. The topic of correctional institutions is so broad that it would be impossible to write a comprehensive thesis on this topic; you must remember to keep your topic area narrow. The topic of correctional institutions can be reduced into subcategories, including (but not limited to): offenders, correctional officers, classes/programs (e.g., education), medical issues (e.g., spreading of AIDS), religion, treatment, violence in prison, and staff training. Now assume that you decide to study issues related to offenders and religion. You want to know about how religion affects prisoners, issues related to religious conversion of inmates in prison, and how this relates to offender recidivism. There is a lot of information on this topic, it is narrow in scope, and you should be able to write a comprehensive literature review on this topic. Now that you know the topic, you can begin to find what has already been written about it.

INFORMATION SOURCES

Numerous sources exist for you to find information on your research topic. It is important that you find sources that are not just relevant, but also academically credible. The two most common credible sources of information are books and journal articles. You may also find information on your topic in newspapers, on the Internet, in magazines, or in other forms such as on flyers. However, much of this information is not held to any academic rigor and therefore may be questionable in several ways. If you are going to use information from one of these sources, you should consider certain factors.

To begin with, it is necessary to distinguish whether the article is based upon opinion or fact. Sometimes this question is easy to answer; for instance, most newspaper articles are fact-based, though those in the op-ed section are opinion-based. Magazine articles are often based around facts, but also tend to include the author's opinion about certain issues or slant the article towards its readership. For instance, general interest magazines such as *Atlantic Monthly* are likely to publish articles that are fact-based and issue-based, and entertainment magazines such as *Cosmopolitan* may include articles on topical issues but primarily focus on personal sides of the issue. The reliability of facts in an article may depend upon the quality of investigative reporting in magazines or articles. Thus, although both the *New York Times* and a tabloid may discuss the same issue, such as a violent attack that occurred in the Rikers Island jail, the *Times* article would be more likely to support the story with additional facts and statistics, such as the amount of violence that occurs in prisons annually, number of injuries and/or deaths, and potential causes of the violence. Newspaper and magazine articles may also differ in how they present facts depending upon their political inclinations. Thus, the *New York Times* and the *Wall Street Journal* would be likely to present a story on an issue differently, because the *New York Times* tends to have a more liberal outlook and the *Wall Street Journal* a more conservative one. All of this is also true for Internet articles, though on the Internet you are even more likely to find opinion-based information. You should never (unless specifically told to do so) use information from blogs, discussion boards, or personal websites. These will always contain opinion-based information.

In addition to the type of information provided, it is also important to understand who is the author or the article, and whether the author has an agenda for the article. For example, if you are writing a paper on sexual offenders and you search the Internet for information, you may find several websites hosted by the parents of children who were sexually abused or murdered, such as the Klaas Kids website. Polly Klaas was abducted from her home and sexually abused and killed by a sexual predator; her father, Mark Klaas, now keeps an updated website of issues related to sexual offenders. Although he includes many facts on his website and links to other useful websites, such as state sex offender registries, he also keeps journals and personal information on the website to share with readers.

Books and Journal Articles

Although all of these limitations are relevant to any type of information source, books and journal articles are usually held to a higher standard of academic rigor than other sources of information. As such, these are usually good places to begin your search for information.

An assignment that requires a literature review will most likely seek your basic understanding of the broad range of material on a particular topic, as well as information on studies conducted in this field. Books are more likely to provide you with general information on a topic. There are three primary types of books you may find when searching for information on criminal justice issues: novels, "true crime" books, and academic books (based upon research). A search may result in hits on all of these types of books. For instance, if you are writing a literature review on serial killers, a search will produce a wide variety of suggested books that include fictitious crime novels (e.g., Patricia Cornwall's *Blowfly*), "true crime" thrillers based upon real serial killer cases (e.g., Ann Rule's *The Stranger Beside Me*, about Ted Bundy), and research-based books (e.g., John Douglas's *Mind Hunter*). When sorting through this vast array of information, you can begin by eliminating the novels and the true crime books. Though interesting and likely inclusive of actual facts on this topic, they will not provide the type of structured, fact-based information you are seeking. You want to focus solely on academic books that are based upon research. These contain features such as a bibliography, citations throughout the text, research-based facts, and an analysis of the issues.

Though they provide less general information, journal articles will provide you with current research information on any topic. The information in journal articles is more current than that in books, because journals release multiple editions each year. These multiple editions, on average four per year, combine to make one volume per year. Because journals have multiple publications throughout the year , they contain current, timely data on research topics. Thus, if you look up an article on search and seizure you may find the following article in *Criminology and Public Policy*.

Gould, J. B. & Mastrofski, S. D. (2004). Suspect searches: Assessing police behavior under the U.S. Constitution. *Criminology & Public Policy*, 3(3): 315–362.

This means that the article is in the third volume and it is in the third edition.

Like books, all journals are not of the same quality. They can be divided into two types of journals: those that are peer-reviewed and those that are non-peer-reviewed. When a journal is peer-reviewed, it means that before an article is accepted for publication, it must be reviewed, usually anonymously, by other academics within the same field. These academics suggest that the article be accepted as is, that it be accepted with revisions, or that it be rejected. This is a high academic standard; in fact, the peer-reviewed journal article is the highest standard of academic publication, and a good source of research information for your literature review.

Most journal articles follow a consistent format, whether presenting quantitative or qualitative data. This basic format is: brief literature review, methodology (including aims and objective, hypothesis, sample, and method of data collection), results (including tables, figures and charts), and the analysis (including limitations to the study design). The next issue to understand is what kind of information is provided in the article: quantitative or qualitative research, or both.

Empirical Research: Distinguishing Between Quantitative and Qualitative Data

The aim of empirical research is to answer questions through objective observation. The way this observation is conducted varies, thus producing different types of data. When you read journal articles that provide statistical information, these articles are providing you with quantitative data. If the articles offer descriptive information, they are providing you with qualitative data. Both quantitative and qualitative data are derived from empirical research and are valid forms of information that are useful for a literature review. Both enhance the understanding of the field and complement each other in terms of the information provided.

Quantitative data is usually derived from some type of experimental research method. Empirical research that is experimental in nature, or attempts to explain a causal relationship between multiple variables, generally follows scientific method. Scientific method consists of four components: first, the researcher must make a general observation or state a hypothesis; second, the researcher must develop a theoretical understanding of the issue; third, the researchers must collect data through careful, detailed observations; and finally, the researcher must take the data, analyze it, and revise the original hypothesis or observation. This type of research is *deductive* in nature; in other words, the researcher begins with a hypothesis and collects data to support or falsify a hypothesis.

Hypotheses are statements explaining the relationships between two or more variables, called the *dependent variable* and *independent variable*. The dependent variable is what is being measured. The independent variable is something that can have an influence on what is being measured. There must be a dependent variable and at least one independent variable in a hypothesis. Changes in the independent variable (cause) predict changes in the dependent variable (effect). For instance, if you are reading a deductive study on fear of crime and the media, the hypothesis may be that individuals who watch the news (cause) are more fearful of crime (effect) than those who do not.

Surveys are perhaps the most common form of data collection, and are often used to gather data for quantitative analysis. Surveys are written questionnaires that are sent or given to people, usually large samples, to ask a given set of questions. The purpose of the survey is to compare answers among people within the sample. Though surveys take many forms, they most often contain questions with yes/no answers or questions that require a response on a *Likert scale.* A Likert scale offers a range of 5–7 answers for the reader, from very low to very high, strongly agree to strongly disagree, and so on. These answers are then coded and analyzed statistically.

Surveys are not the only form of data collection for quantitative articles, however. Another method of data collection is documentary analysis, which is the examination of written documents such as books, reports, records, crime rates, and so on. Researchers use documentary analysis when they want information on what has already been written or gathered. For instance, a researcher studying recidivism rates amongst prisoners with behavioral problems in prison would have to look at prisoners' records, including disciplinary records, in order to understand the behavioral problems of the prisoners.

Studies do not always begin with a hypothesis and surveys are not always used as a means to gather data. With *inductive* research, the aim is to find out all information possible about a particular topic. This is descriptive data, and such inductive studies do not begin with a hypothesis but use the data to induce inferences. Usually this type of descriptive study produces qualitative data. Quantitative studies may use surveys to gather data; qualitative studies are more likely to utilize interviews or ethnographic methods of data gathering. Interviews are useful if you want to find out more information than that which can be offered on a survey. For instance, if you want to find out about why prisoners committed their offenses, you may not get all the information you need by sending them surveys. However, by interviewing them, you can ask a given set of questions, along with follow-up questions that help to clarify their answers.

Ethnography, or the study of individuals or groups in a particular area, is another method of qualitative data collection. Researchers conduct an ethnographic study if they want to observe how people live or behave regularly, often becoming part of the community that they are observing. Many anthropological studies are ethnographic, as anthropologists study the origin, the behavior, and the cultural development of groups or populations. Criminologists can also conduct ethnographic research, however. Examples would include studies that aim to understand drug or gang culture, where the researcher lives surrounded by individuals who are in gangs or using, selling, or manufacturing drugs in order to better understand them as individuals and as members of a particular group.

Documentary analysis can be used for qualitative research as well. Going back to the earlier example, a researcher may want to study the recidivism rates of prisoners who had disciplinary problems in prison. The researcher can read the prison records to understand the scope of their problems in prison, but qualitative researchers can utilize this same information to better understand the nature of the problem.

Many times researchers use multiple methods of data collection and analysis, or a *triangulation* of research methods. This enhances the data and also may compensate for the deficiencies of a particular research method by supporting it with information derived from another source. So, for instance, for a longitudinal study with a cohort of prisoners who converted to religion in prison, a researcher could collect data in multiple ways. First, the researcher can send prisoners surveys at the outset of the study to collect information regarding their demographics (such as age, marital status, religion, etc.) and offense background. Next, the researcher can interview a subset of the prisoners to understand more fully their views on prison, their offenses, why they converted, and so forth. Subsequently, the researcher can interview them to find out about their lives upon their release from prison, including whether they remained converted and whether they have committed any offenses. Then, to support the data from the interviews, the researcher can conduct documentary analysis by searching for any arrest and conviction data.

EXAMPLES OF QUANTITATIVE AND QUALITATIVE STUDIES

Often, multiple studies have been done on any single research topic. Some are quantitative studies and others qualitative studies. By looking at some criminal justice research topics, you can see the different type of information produced by quantitative and qualitative research. Following are examples of what you may find in journals:

- *Drug use.* In a qualitative study, the researcher may interview prisoners who were convicted of drug offenses to understand how and why they began using illegal drugs. In a quantitative study, the researcher may hypothesize that cocaine users in New York City are more likely than heroin users to commit violent offenses. The study would collect information to show statistical differences in violent offense rates between heroin and cocaine users.
- *Religion in prison.* In a qualitative study, the researcher may ask inmates about why they had a religious conversion in prison, and their experiences before and after this conversion. In a quantitative study, the researcher may analyze offenders released from prison and compare recidivism rates amongst those who did and those who did not have a religious conversion in prison.
- *Police/community relationship.* In a qualitative study, the researcher may go to neighborhoods of various socioeconomic statuses and observe the interactions, both formal and informal, between residents and the police. The qualitative researcher may also hold focus groups with a small number of residents to find out more about how they felt during those interactions. In a quantitative study, the researcher may analyze complaints against the police and compare rates of complaints amongst neighborhoods.
- *Crime rates.* In a qualitative study, the researcher may speak to "career criminals" in prison to understand the extent of their criminal behavior over time, how their criminal behavior evolved, and general questions about why they did not desist from criminal behavior. In a

quantitative study, the researcher may evaluate crime trend data over a period of years and attempt to understand what factors may lead to an increase or decrease in criminal activity.

• *Prison and families.* In a qualitative study, researchers may speak to women in prison and their children to find out how prison has affected their family relationships. In a quantitative study, the researcher may survey high-crime neighborhoods to find out how many family members or friends are in or have been in prison, and analyze the impact of this on the neighborhood economically.

Though by absolutely no means exhaustive, these examples show how both quantitative and qualitative research can be conducted on a single topic, and in each of the example situations, both the quantitative and qualitative studies mentioned can be utilized together to better understand the issue.

Though the topics to be studied in the field of criminal justice are endless, all studies are not conducted to the highest methodological standards. As you conduct your literature review, you need to be able to understand the benefits of the research studies you are reading as well as the flaws in the studies. You should be able to not just summarize what you are reading, but also critically analyze the articles. You are highly likely to read articles, particularly quantitative articles, that present conflicting results of studies, and you need to be able to understand why this is the case and which article is of a higher standard.

RESEARCH LIMITATIONS

No project is perfect, and all studies have limitations. As you conduct a literature review, you need to be able to recognize and understand these limitations. Some common problems with research articles are as follows.

• *Sample.* The sample is the population that the researcher studied. It is usually difficult to measure the entire population, or the *universe,* so most researchers utilize a small selection of individuals within the whole population. There are four main types of samples in criminal justice research: the random sample (this is usually the best form of sampling to get a representative group from within a population); systematic selection (such as choosing every third, fifth, tenth person, etc., in a sample); nonprobability sampling (a purposive sample chosen because of certain characteristics, such as all drivers with red cars in a neighborhood); and snowballing (building a sample based upon others in the sample, such as friends of friends).

You must understand what the sample is in the study (e.g., groups, organizations, populations, or individuals) and then assess the quality of the sample. There are two common problems with sampling: the size and the representativeness. Sample size is often a limitation with research projects. The sample needs to be large enough to make accurate conclusions, but not so large that it is unmanageable. This is especially difficult with qualitative data, which may include interviews. If the sample is not large enough (generally, at least 100 subjects in a quantitative study), the research will not be generalizable (applicable to the population being studied). The sample must also be representative of the population studied. If the study is assessing burglars, and the researcher took a sample of 200 men imprisoned for burglary, is this representative of all burglars? Even though the size of the sample is adequate, it will not be representative, because it is only looking at those burglars who were caught, arrested, convicted, and incarcerated.

• *Variable definitions.* Many studies define their variables differently. You need to be aware of how the researcher defines the variables, because unless variables are defined to be the same, they are not comparable. For instance, if you are reading about recidivism of violent offenders, how does the researcher define recidivism? It can be defined variably as being convicted of another violent offense, being convicted of any other offense, being arrested for a violent or any offense, or committing but not being arrested or convicted for another offense, and so on. Studies that define recidivism differently will produce distinctly different statistics for this phenomenon. Take, for example, an offender convicted of manslaughter; when is he a recidivist? Is it when he is arrested again for any offense, convicted for any offense, arrested or convicted for murder/nonnegligent manslaughter, or arrested or convicted for a violent offense? How the variables are defined will have a significant effect on the study outcome. If the researcher defines recidivism as any arrest, this will result in a much higher rate of recidivism than if the researcher defines it as just being convicted for the same offense again.

- **Time dimension.** Though not a limitation, the time dimension of the study will have an effect on the type of information provided. There are two primary types of studies in terms of time dimensions: *cross-sectional* studies and *longitudinal* studies. Cross-sectional studies are like taking a photograph of a situation at one point in time. Researchers conduct cross-sectional research when they want to find a one-time answer to a question. For instance, to find out which state had the highest rate of robbery in 2003, you could look at crime rates of all states and answer that question. Longitudinal studies, on the other hand, look at situations over a period of time. There are two ways in which this can be accomplished: through trend data or by following a cohort. With trend data, you look at information over a period of time. For instance, you can follow robbery trends over a 10-year period in the Uniform Crime Reports. With a cohort, the researcher follows a group over a period of time, such as a cohort of juveniles throughout high school to see differences in crime rates within the group. Cross-sectional and longitudinal studies produce different types of data, and it is important to understand the difference when summarizing the information in the literature review.

- **Exogenous/intervening variables.** Variables other than the independent variable may affect the dependent variable, thus altering what you are measuring. The researcher should account for these, but may not be able to do so. So, for instance, if looking at those with religious conversions in prison, the researcher may include in the sample prisoners who also had a number of other factors influence them in prison, such as education, job training, therapy, and so forth. There are certain statistical analyses that take into consideration these factors and measure only what is trying to be measured; however, it is important to understand who is in the sample and all the factors that can cause the effect being measured.

- **Reliability and validity.** Is the study accurately measuring what it says it is? If not, it is not *valid*. Is there consistency in what you are measuring? If not, the study is not reliable. If the researcher tests the effect of exogenous variables, the results are not valid. If the researcher's study results cannot be replicated, then the findings are not reliable. For instance, have any other researchers conducted a similar study? If the researcher has used a survey instrument, has it been validated? These are important issues to understand.

THE ANNOTATED BIBLIOGRAPHY

Though for some topics the relevant literature is not extensive, in many cases there are dozens, if not hundreds, of books and articles on a single topic area. The literature review must have a logical structure, with material clearly integrated by topic area. Because all of this material is often difficult to organize, it may help you to prepare for the literature review by compiling an *annotated bibliography*. An annotated bibliography is a system of taking notes on all books and articles that you read on a topic and compiling a bibliography with brief explanations for each reference. Because this is used only for your reference, it does not need to be in a particular format and does not need to be written in full, complete sentences. Here is an example of how to incorporate information from the article discussed previously from the journal *Criminology & Public Policy*:

> Gould, J. B. & Mastrofski, S. D. (2004). Suspect searches: Assessing police behavior under the U.S. Constitution. *Criminology & Public Policy*, 3(3): 315–362.
>
> - Lit review goes over classic articles on policing and right to stop and search as well as aggressive policing tactics (e.g., Wilson and Kelling, Goldstein, Klockars, Skolnick, Reiss). Previous studies show conflicting results regarding stats on whether police follow correct constitutional procedures when stopping and searching.
> - Methodology: direct observation of police officers over a three-month period in stop/search activities. Benefit to this methodology = most accurate and objective; Problem = may produce bias in officer reactions (may be more likely to behave appropriately due to observer). Also, only looked at one jurisdiction, no comparison/generalization.
> - Findings: 30% of sample searched unconstitutionally; 18% arrested unconstitutionally, 45.5% of pat downs were unconstitutional (pg. 333).
> - Tables pp. 339, 342–343 show regression analyses. Show that other than age, no factors show that illegal searches are socially biased.

The key issues that you want to note in the annotated bibliography are the purpose of the study, the methodology, and the findings; note the page numbers that might be useful if you need to reference the article. It may be helpful for you to write this in bullet-point form for easy reference, as in the previous example.

You can structure an annotated bibliography in a number of ways. If there are few subsections of the essay, you can simply structure it alphabetically. For example, if your assignment is to summarize all journal articles in the last 10 years that relate to social bonding theory, then it may be best to simply find the articles and write the annotated bibliography alphabetically. On the other hand, if your assignment calls for a discussion about the development of laws related to search and seizure since the 1960s, then the annotated bibliography will be more useful if divided into subsections. To write about search and seizure laws since the 1960s would include case law information on persons and places, and more specifically of homes, cars, workplaces, public transportation vehicles, airports, roadblocks, open fields, phones, and the Internet. Additionally, you would have to write about the constitutionality of searches and how they are limited depending upon race (e.g., racial profiling), location of the object searched (e.g., whether it was in plain view), standards of searching (e.g., what constitutes probable cause or reasonable suspicion), and exigent circumstances (emergency searches). Finally, you would have to include a discussion of landmark cases and their effect on the system. This would be a very onerous assignment without an organized plan by which to study such facts, and the best way is to organize the annotated bibliography into sections based upon these major topics. By organizing all of your information at the outset, you will be better able to write a comprehensive review of all relevant literature.

SUMMARIZING THE LITERATURE

Once you have read all relevant articles and books on this topic, you are ready to begin writing the literature review. You have already gathered the necessary information and organized it into an annotated bibliography. The next thing that you need to do is write an outline. An outline is an organizational structure for your paper. It is *always* best to begin a literature review, or any research paper, with an outline. Unless told otherwise, the literature review has the same structure as other essays you have written in the past: introduction, body, conclusion. However, with the literature review you will likely have several subsections within the body and you will have to organize the information in a structured way. As an example, consider a literature review on complaints against the police. You could have an outline that is as follows:

I. Introduction
II. Number of complaints against the police in the United States
    A. Number of officers with complaints historically and today
    B. Who files complaints against the police
III. Nature of the complaints against the police in the United States
    A. "Minor" offenses (e.g., verbal abuse)
    B. Major offenses (e.g., police brutality)
IV. "Policing the police": how complaints are handled
    A. Internal affairs bureau
    B. External review boards
        1. Development of the boards
        2. Benefits to external review
        3. Problems with external review
V. International comparison of complaints against the police
VI. Conclusion

Once you have the outline, you can begin to incorporate information from the annotated bibliography. You want to make sure that as you are writing the literature review you synthesize the information, or integrate all of the information on a given topic. A common problem in literature reviews is that students simply summarize one reference at a time, describing what one author wrote, followed by another and another. This information is merely a description of what has been written and is what you want to avoid. A synthesis of the information requires you to analyze similarities and differences in what multiple authors say about a topic. For instance, on the topic of complaints against the police, you could have a paragraph on the implementation of civilian review boards that is as follows:

> The primary reason the police were opposed to the initiation of civilian review boards was that they were offended by the notion that their actions would be judged by individuals removed from the situations which they encountered on a daily basis (Goldstein, 1977). They considered the civilian review boards to be an "unwarranted political interference in police affairs" (Brown, 1983, p. 16), and they believed that such a model of review would eliminate a large percentage of the initiative, aggressiveness and necessary discretion that is the basis of police work. Police saw the law as a double-edged sword: they were its enforcers, and at the same time subject to its judgment (Kerstetter, 1995, p. 260). It was feared that the people who made complaints (the "assholes," according to Van Maanan, 1978) would be considered more credible than officers when relating accounts of events, thereby undermining the role

of the officers and their moral superiority. They felt that in order to understand the discretion that is crucial to the job and requires an officer to deviate from exact written rules of the law, one must have had experience in the job (Reiner, 1993).

> Source: Terry, K. J. & Grant, H. (2004). The roads not taken: Improving the use of civilian complaint review boards and implementation of the recommendations from investigative commissions. In D. Jones-Brown and K. Terry (Eds.), *Policing and minority communities: Bridging the gap* (pp. 160–182). Upper Saddle River, NJ: Prentice Hall.

This paragraph incorporates the work of five researchers. It is synthesized; it does not describe paragraph by paragraph what each one said, but rather integrates what all of them said about this topic into one paragraph. You should continue to synthesize information throughout the paper in this way.

Summary

When writing a literature review, it is best to approach this task systematically. A literature review is a summary of what has already been written about a particular topic. You will find this information in books, journal articles, and sometimes on the Internet, in newspapers, or in magazines. For longer papers, it may help to begin with an annotated bibliography, or a bullet-point summary of what you have read organized by author or subtopic. Your literature review for a criminal justice topic will most likely incorporate information that is both quantitative and qualitative in nature. It is important to understand and recognize high-quality research studies, giving more weight in your analysis to those that are methodologically sound and have fewer limitations. The literature review should be more than a simple description of what exists; it should provide an analysis of what has been studied, recognizing the gaps in the research and what type of research should thus be conducted on this topic in the future.

References

Brown, D. C. (1983). *Civilian review of complaints against the police: A survey of the United States literature*. London, England: Home Office Research and Planning Unit, H.M.S.O.

Clarke, R.V. (ed.). (1997). *Situational crime prevention: Successful case studies* (2nd ed.). New York, NY: Harrow and Heston.

Cohen, L. E. & Felson, M. (1979). Social changes and crime rate trends: A routine activities approach. *American Sociological Review*, 44(4): 588–608.

Goldstein, H. (1977). *Policing a free society*. Cambridge, MA: Ballinger.

Kerstetter, W. A. (1995). A "procedural justice" perspective on police and citizen satisfaction with investigations of police use of force: Finding a common ground of fairness. In W. A. Geller and H. Toch (Eds.), *And Justice For All: Understanding and Controlling Police Abuse of Force*. Washington, DC: Police Executive Research Forum.

Reiner, R. (1993). *The politics of the police* (2nd ed). Sussex, England: Wheatsheat Books Ltd.

Terry, K. & Grant, H. (2004). The roads not taken: Improving the use of civilian complaint review boards and implementation of the recommendations from investigative commissions. In D. Jones-Brown and K. Terry (Eds.), *Policing and minority communities: Bridging the gap*. Upper Saddle River, NJ: Prentice Hall.

Van Maanen, J. (1978). The asshole. In P. Manning and J. Van Maanen (Eds.), *Policing: A view from the street*. New York, NY: Random House.

9 | REFERENCES: SEARCHING FOR AND CITING SOURCES

Finding and citing sources of information is an important part of any research paper. There are many types of sources, such as books, journal articles, and the Internet, and the method of referencing them in a research paper depends largely upon the discipline. Because writing in criminal justice is an interdisciplinary endeavor, there is no single method of referencing material. The purpose of this chapter is to review the various sources of information, where to find them, and the ways in which students may be asked to cite them.

LOCATING SOURCES IN THE LIBRARY

Most research papers will require the student to find information on a particular topic and summarize it in a literature review, as discussed in Chapter 8. The main sources of academic information are books and journal articles. Most university libraries use a uniform system of categorizing books called the Library of Congress Classification system. This system uses call numbers to categorize books by subject. The full list of topics categorized in this system can be found online at http://www. loc.gov/catdir/cpso/lcco/lcco.html.

Books that relate to the social sciences are categories under the call letters of H. However, "social sciences" covers a broad range of topics and can be further broken down into "subclasses," as seen in Table 9.1.

Not all of the social science subclasses are relevant to the study of criminal justice. The most common call number for books on crime, criminals, and justice can be found in the library under call numbers beginning with HM (sociology), HN (social problems), HQ (the family, marriage, and women, including material related to sexual behavior and abuse), and HV (social pathology, social and public welfare, and criminology). These subclasses can be broken down further into specific topics. Table 9.2 shows the topics that relate to criminology within the HV subclass. Note that the HV 6000 series of books is related to criminology, HV 7000 is related to criminal justice administration, and HV 8000 and 9000 are related to specific institutions (police and corrections).

Although books related to criminology and most of the social sciences are located under the call number of H, it is important to remember that many criminal justice resources are also located within other topic areas. For instance, books with the topic of law are located under the call number of K (Constitutional Law located in K3154-3370 and Criminal Law and Procedure is located under K5000-5582); psychology under B (subclass BF); and anthropology under G (subclass GN).

Call number Subclass	Topic
	Table 9.1 Categories of books in the social sciences, by call number subclass.
H	Social sciences (General).
HA	Statistics.
HB	Economic theory. Demography.
HC	Economic history and conditions.
HD	Industries. Land use, Labor.
HE	Transportation and communications.
HF	Commerce.
HG	Finance.
HJ	Public finance.
HM	Sociology (General).
HN	Social history, conditions. Social problems. Social reform.
HQ	The family. Marriage. Women.
HS	Societies: secret, benevolent, etc.
HT	Communities. Classes. Races.
HV	Social pathology. Social and public welfare. Criminology.
HX	Socialism. Communism.

Source: Library of Congress Classification System at http://www.loc.gov/catdir/cpso/lcco/lcco.html.

The grouping of books with the same subject under the same or adjacent call numbers makes possible the longtime scholarly pastime of browsing the open stacks of a library. Though this pastime has been partly superceded by Internet browsing, the absence of older texts and whole book texts on the Internet makes stack browsing still popular. Once you see that you are looking for books at certain call numbers, you may discover useful titles you did not know to seek out by browsing through the books at the same exact call number or the adjacent ones.

Though many journal articles can now be found online, they can also be found in a library. Journals are classified under the same call system as books. They are located based upon the title of the journal, not the journal article. The highest-ranking journals in the field of criminal justice and criminology, as indicated by their impact factors, are listed in Table 9.3, along with journals in topics related to the criminal justice field.[1]

When looking up journal articles, it is common to use electronic information databases at the university by typing in the title, author, or keyword. Many university libraries have their own electronic system through which students can search for journal articles. However, there are some uniform databases for journal articles that are commonly used in universities across the country. Examples of such databases in criminal justice are Criminal Justice Abstracts, Criminal Justice Periodical Index, NCJRS Abstracts Database, or Full Text Resources. For sociology, the premier engines are socINDEX and sociology abstracts. For psychology, the most common search engines are psyclit, psycINFO, pscyhARTCILES, psycBOOKS, and psycEXTRA. Also, it is possible to find

---

[1]Rankings of journals can be determined in a number of ways, the most common of which are through "impact factors." The impact factor of a journal is a calculation based the average number of times articles in the journal are cited for approximately two years after publication. The journals listed in Table 9.3 have the highest impact factors in the field of criminal justice research as of 2006.

Table 9.2 Subclass of HV call numbers, as they relate to criminology.

Call number classification	Topic
HV6001-7220.5	Criminology.
HV6035-6197	Criminal anthropology, including criminal types, criminal psychology, prison psychology, causes of crime.
HV6201-6249	Criminal classes.
HV6250-6250.4	Victims of crimes. Victimology.
HV6251-6773.55	Crimes and offenses.
HV6774-7220.5	Crimes and criminal classes.
HV7231-9960	Criminal justice administration.
HV7428	Social work with delinquents and criminals.
HV7431	Prevention of crime, methods, etc.
HV7435-7439	Gun control.
HV7551-8280.7	Police. Detectives. Constabulary.
HV7935-8025	Administration and organization.
HV8031-8080	Police duty. Methods of protection.
HV8035-8069	Special classes of crimes, offenses, and criminals.
HV8073-8079.35	Investigation of crimes. Examination and identification of prisoners.
HV8079.2-8079.35	Police social work.
HV8079.5-8079.55	Traffic control. Traffic accident investigation.
HV8081-8099	Private detectives. Detective bureaus.
HV8130-8280.7	By region or country.
HV8290-8291	Private security services.
HV8301-9920.7	Penology. Prisons. Corrections.
HV9051-9230.7	The juvenile offender. Juvenile delinquency. Reform schools, etc.
HV9261-9430.7	Reformation and reclamation of adult prisoners.
HV9441-9920.7	By region or country.
HV9950-9960	By region or country.

Source: Library of Congress Classification System at http://www.loc.gov/catdir/cpso/lcco/lcco.html.

criminal justice–related articles on search engines such as MEDLINE and SCOPUS, which, although linked to science and medical topics, may overlap with topics in the criminal justice field. Many of these specific search engines are incorporated in larger, general search engines, such as EBSCOhost Academic Search. EBSCO allows for a search of several engines that span the social sciences, allowing for a more expansive search. Once you identify an article through the search engine, there are two ways in which you can retrieve the article. If the university library subscribes to the journal online, then you can click on and download the article. If not, you can identify the journal article title, the journal it is in, the volume number and issue number of the journal, and also find the hard copy of the journal in the library.

To illustrate this search process for both books and journal articles, consider that you are asked to write a 10-page literature review on domestic violence. The assignment requires students

Table 9.3 Top-ranking journals in the field of criminal justice.

Discipline	Journal
Criminal Justice/ Criminology	*British Journal of Criminology*
	Criminal Justice and Behavior
	Crime & Delinquency
	Criminology
	Criminology & Public Policy
	Journal of Criminal Law & Criminology
	Journal of Quantitative Criminology
	Journal of Research in Crime & Delinquency
	Justice Quarterly
	Theoretical Criminology
Sociology	*American Journal of Sociology*
	American Sociological Review
	Social Problems
Psychology/Human Behavior	*Behavioral Sciences & the Law*
	Law and Human Behavior
	Psychology, Public Policy and Law

to include an overview of the topic as well as of up-to-date research on criminal justice policy. Books are likely to give you more general information about domestic violence. As you search through the university's online catalog, you decide that books such as *The Domestic Violence Handbook* (New York State Coalition Against Domestic Violence) and *Domestic Violence: The Criminal Justice Response* (Sage) would be good places to begin, providing the reader with general information on what domestic violence is, whom it affects, and what the criminal justice system has done in response to domestic violence.

Because journal articles tend to include more up-to-date research than books, you then look for journal articles on this topic. The topic of domestic violence spans several disciplines; criminal justice policy articles would be included in criminal justice journals, and causes and effects of domestic violence might be covered in sociology and psychology journals. Looking first through criminal justice abstracts, you type in keywords "domestic violence." Even when narrowing down this topic to include only articles in the last two years, over 3000 articles appear. It is, however, possible to narrow down the general topic of "domestic violence" so that there are fewer hits and the list becomes more manageable to search.

The assignment states that you need to include up-to-date research on criminal justice policy and domestic violence. Instead of simply typing in "domestic violence" like this:

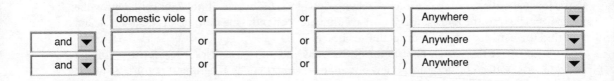

You can narrow it down by typing in additional words like this:

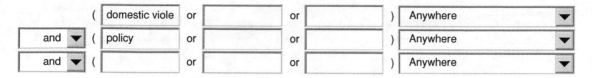

This still produces more than 300 matches, and it is possible to narrow it down even further by typing in additional keywords (police policy, sentencing, etc.).

Another type of scholarly database that can be used is JSTOR. JSTOR, which stands for Journal Storage, is a journal archive of more than 300 scholarly journals. It serves as a database for all articles published in these journals. However, it does not publish the most recent articles, or those published between one and five years ago, as those are generally accessible in libraries and online. The purpose of JSTOR is to ensure that all scholarly articles published over the years are accessible. Scholarly articles on many topics are available through JSTOR: it is not specific to the field of criminal justice. However, the field of criminal justice is represented with journals such as the *Journal of Criminal Justice and Criminology* and *Crime and Justice.*

Perhaps the most extensive database for social science research information is the Inter-University Consortium for Political and Social Research (ICPSR) (located at http://www.icpsr. umich.edu, if not through the university library). Based at the University of Michigan, ICPSR provides access to a vast archive of social science data. The purpose of ICPSR is to preserve data, storing datasets on a variety of criminal justice-related topics. ICPSR also provides support researchers at the more than 500 research universities associated with the organization. This support can assist the researcher in identifying relevant data for analysis. Unlike most of the electronic databases, ICPSR supplies actual datasets collected in social science research, generally in the forms of SAS, SPSS (Statistical Packages for the Social Sciences), and Stata. This database can be used for more sophisticated research papers, and may not be appropriate for the average, introductory undergraduate criminal justice class.

One of the more common scholarly databases in the field of criminal justice and, in particular, law, is LexisNexis.[2] LexisNexis is a user-friendly legal search engine. Like the criminal justice search engines, it is necessary to subscribe to LexisNexis in order to use it. Most universities that have legal and/or criminal justice classes subscribe to LexisNexis. Using this search engine, it is possible to search for the following type of information:

- Secondary Information (legal news and articles)
- Case Law (searchable by name and citation)
- Codes and Regulations
- International Legal Material
- Patent Research
- Career Information

The most useful information for the criminal justice student will come from the first two categories: Secondary Information and Case Law. In Secondary Information, it is possible to search for any articles related to legal news, which encompasses many criminal justice issues.

---

[2]Some universities will instead, or also, have Westlaw, an alternative legal database. Westlaw, produced by Thompson, is a more advanced system than the academic version of LexisNexis and is used by many law firms.

Similarly, the legal articles under secondary information are those published in law reviews and relate to legal analyses of criminal justice issues.

In order to understand how the Lexis search engine works, assume that you have been asked to write a paper on the affect of domestic violence policies on children. You would begin by looking up domestic violence and then narrowing down the topic. A search of 2005 law review articles on "domestic violence" produces more than 1,000 articles, so it is necessary to narrow down the topic and restrict the number of articles. So, a search of "domestic violence," narrowed by "policy," produces over 900 articles; narrowed further by "police" produces more than 600 articles; narrowed further by "arrest" produces more than 300 articles; narrowed further by "social services" produces just over 100 articles; narrowed further by "foster care" produces 36 articles; and, finally, narrowed further by "child abuse" produces 29 articles. This means that the 29 articles will all discuss domestic violence issues that contain information on policy, police, arrest, foster care, and child abuse. These 29 articles are a good place to start reading about the effect of domestic violence on children.

SEARCHING THE INTERNET AND PUBLIC DATABASES

Though the search engines mentioned are some of the most useful academic sources, many require paid subscriptions and are often accessible only through a university. Even universities vary in which electronic information databases they offer. Even without these databases, it is possible to conduct academic research using the Internet. But be careful: when conducting academic research, it is important to access only information that is either from official sites (e.g., the National Institute of Justice) or that contains legitimate research findings. It is important to avoid subjective articles, or those that simply support the opinions of the writers. If you do utilize sources that are clearly from a subjective source, it is important to identify this in the paper you are writing and, if possible, to supplement this information with objective facts or information that presents the opposite viewpoint of the issue.

There is a broad list of Internet resources that can be used to research criminal justice topics. The following list, which is not exhaustive, is a good start:

- *The National Criminal Justice Reference Service (NCJRS):* http://www.ncjrs.gov. According to the website, NCJRS is a federally funded resource offering justice and substance abuse information to support research, policy, and program development worldwide. NCJRS is the most extensive resource of criminal justice-related articles on the Internet, and is funded (in part) by the Office of Justice Programs (which includes the Office of the Assistant Attorney General, the Community Capacity Development Office, the Office of the Police Corps, the Bureau of Justice Assistance, the Bureau of Justice Statistics, National Institute of Justice, Office for Victims of Crime, and the Office of Juvenile Justice and Delinquency Prevention), the Office on Violence Against Women, the National Institute of Corrections, and the Office of Community Policing Services. Articles can be viewed online or purchased.
- *National Institute of Justice (NIJ):* http://nij.ncjrs.org/publications/pubs_db.asp. This is the website for NIJ publications. NIJ funds a large amount of empirical research and many of the publications related to this research can be found here. NIJ upholds a high standard for research and this is an excellent site to search for articles on various criminal justice topics.
- *Bureau of Justice Statistics (BJS):* http://www.ojp.usdoj.gov/bjs/. This is a premier site in which the research can find official statistics related to Crime and Victims, Law Enforcement,

Prosecution, the Federal Justice System, Criminal Offenders, Courts and Sentencing, Special Topics (e.g., drugs, homicide, firearms, and so on), Corrections, Expenditure and Employments (in the criminal justice system), and Criminal Record Systems. The link to their extensive list of publications is http://www.ojp.usdoj.gov/bjs/pubalp2.htm.

- *Office of Juvenile Justice and Delinquency Prevention (OJJDP):* http://ojjdp.ncjrs.org. This website provides information about all aspects of crime and delinquency as it relates to juveniles, including the victimization of children and delinquent acts committed by juveniles. It contains statistical reports as well as links to publications of research funded by OJJDP.

- *Office for Victims of Crime (OVC):* http://www.ovc.gov. The goal of OVC is to oversee programs that benefit victims of crime. They provide funding to state victim assistance and compensation programs, provide training to criminal justice professionals, and fund research to assist in the knowledge of victimization.

- *Office on Violence against Women (OVW):* http://www.usdoj.gov/ovw/. An office of the U.S. Department of Justice, OVW aims to conduct research and implement policy to reduce violence against women, particularly in the areas of domestic violence, dating violence, sexual assault, and stalking. Publications of research funded by OVW are accessible through NCJRS.

- *FBI Uniform Crime Reports (UCR):* http://www.fbi.gov/ucr/ucr.htm. This site provides national crime data. The UCR, instituted by the FBI in 1930, is an annual publication of crime rates nationally. It is the oldest system of recording crime in the United States, and the main focus is on index crimes (murder, rape, robbery, assault, burglary, larceny, motor vehicle theft, and arson). The local police agencies or state agencies give their crime data to the FBI, who tabulates the data on a national level.

- *The VERA Institute of Justice:* http://www.vera.org. VERA is a nonprofit organization devoted to research in criminal justice. Best known for the "Manhattan Bail Project," the goal of this institution is to conduct empirical research about the criminal justice system, with a focus on equity within the system. The VERA website provides information about all of their ongoing projects as well as recent publications and links to a myriad of other criminal justice sites. Research topics cover the areas of crime and victimization, policing, the judicial process, sentencing, and corrections.

- *Urban Institute of Justice (UI):* http://www.urban.org. UI is a research organization that focuses on social and economic policy. Though UI researchers conduct empirical research on a broad range of topics within the criminal justice system, they specialize in issues related to corrections, and in particular, prisoner reentry. The list of their most recent publications is accessible directly through http://www.urban.org/justice/index.cfm.

- *Institute for Law and Justice (ILJ):* http://www.ilj.org. The focus of ILJ is on research on and evaluation of violence, policing, and technology as it relates to the criminal justice field. Researchers at ILJ have completed more than 250 research projects, with findings accessible on this website.

- *Rand Corporation:* http://www.rand.org/justice_area/. RAND, which stands for research and development, is a nonprofit "think tank" responsible for conducting research in a variety of fields. RAND's goal is to provide empirical information that informs policy, with an aim to make the justice system more efficient and more equitable. This website is a link to the publications of RAND researchers in the area of civil justice.

- *American Society of Criminology (ASC):* http://www.asc41.com. The ASC is the primary association for criminologists in the United States and is the publisher of three journals: *Criminology, Criminology & Public Policy,* and *The Criminologist.* This website provides access to information about the organization, including the annual conference and the journals.

- *FindLaw:* http://www.findlaw.com/casecode/. For students who need legal information but do not have access to LexisNexis or Westlaw, FindLaw is a resource that provides information about cases and legislative acts. There is also an online law dictionary available: http://dictionary.lp.findlaw.com.
- *National Center for Victims of Crime (NCVC):* http://www.ncvc.org. NCVC is an advocacy organization for crime victims. Though not a research center, this site does provide links to legislative bills that have been passed related to crime victimization, as well as links to various criminal justice organizations.

CITING REFERENCES

References are the articles and books that you read in order to attain information for an academic paper. *Referencing* refers to the citation of this material both within the paper and in a bibliography. The format of the references will depend upon the type of referencing system the professor asks students to use for a particular class or assignment. There are numerous referencing systems for writing in criminal justice, though the most common referencing style is that of the American Psychological Association, known as APA style referencing (APA, 2001). As such, this is the system discussed in the remainder of this chapter. Even if a professor requests that students use a different referencing system, many of the same principles will apply and it should be simple to adapt to a different system.

APA Referencing Guidelines

APA documentation, like most other citation formats in the social sciences, has two features: a reference list at the end of the paper and in-text citations throughout. In-text citations appear in parentheses at appropriate places in the text and refer to more informative items in the reference list at the end. The reference list is an edited version of the bibliography (the entire list of articles and books you have read for the topic). A reference list differs from a bibliography, which contains readings for background or further study in addition to works cited in the text. Unless told otherwise, you should include a reference list with academic papers, not a bibliography.

FORMAT OF THE REFERENCE LIST

The reference list contains all of the readings cited in the text. There are four primary parts to each reference: the names of the authors; the date; the title of the article, book, or journal; and other publishing information (in this order). Each of the four parts will have a period after it. The author's name is the last name followed by the initial of the first and middle name, if used: for example, Healy, J. F. If there are two or more authors of a publication, names are separated by an ampersand (&): for example, Johnson, M. P. & Ferraro, K. J. If the book is listed under the editor's name, "(Ed.)" appears after the name: Almeida, R. V. (Ed.).

The date of publication appears in parenthesis after the name: (1989). If no date is available, the abbreviation "n.d." is used. Book and journal titles are *italicized.* However, titles of journal articles and book chapters are not italicized, and they come before the title of the journal or book. For journal articles, chapters, and book titles, only the first word of the article or chapter title, and first word of the subtitle if there is one, are capitalized. All words except articles and prepositions in journal titles are capitalized. Book citations include the city and state abbreviation or country name where the book was published and the publisher's name, separated by a colon: Binghamton, NY: Haworth. Journal citations do not include place of publication or publisher, but do include volume and pages. No abbreviation or word for volume or page is used: the first number, the volume, is italicized; the numbers following the comma indicate the pages: *62*, 948–963. If a journal is paginated by issue (that is, if each issue starts with page 1), then the issue number is included in parentheses after the volume number: *3*(1), 124–156. All items on the reference list should have a *hanging indent,* meaning that the first line of the reference is flush left and all subsequent lines are indented. All citations in the reference list should follow this format. Following are some examples of what references will look like in a reference list, taking into consideration all of the above-mentioned factors.

The reference of a book by a single author should look like this:

Warr, M. (2002). *Companions in crime: The social aspects of criminal conduct.* Cambridge, England: Cambridge University Press.

For works with up to seven authors, list all author names with an ampersand before the last name. For works with eight or more authors, list the first six authors, then insert three ellipses, and add the last author's name. Always alphabetize the reference by the last name of the first author (here, Akers). Also note that the following reference includes the notation "(4th ed.)," which means that this is the fourth edition of the book (ed. is also the abbreviation used when a book is edited; however, "Ed." is capitalized for editor and appears immediately after the editor's name).

Akers, R. L. & Sellers, C. S. (2004). *Criminological theory: Introduction, evaluation and application* (4th ed.). Los Angeles, CA: Roxbury Press.

Edited books follow the same format as authored books, alphabetized by the (first) editor's last name with the (Ed.) or (Eds.) notation.

Tonry, M. (Ed.). (2000). *The handbook of crime and punishment.* New York, NY: Oxford University Press.

If there is neither an author nor editor, the article is alphabetized by the first significant word of the title. This occurs often with newspaper and magazine articles. For the in-text citation, you would just use the first significant word or two in the title (in this case, "Perceptions").

Perceptions of child sexual abuse as a public health problem—September 1995 (August 29, 1997). *Morbidity and Mortality Weekly Report, Centers for Disease Control and Prevention, 46*(34), 801–803.

If there is more than one work cited by the same author or authors, they are listed chronologically from the earliest to the most recent. If two or more works by the same author or authors appeared in the same year, they are arranged by alphabetizing the first significant word of the title and given a letter following the date of publication, that is, 1988a, 1988b. For example:

Marshall, W. L. (1994). Treatment effects on denial and minimization in incarcerated sex offenders. *Behavior Research and Therapy, 32,* 559–564.

Marshall, W. L. (1996). Assessment, treatment and theorizing about sex offenders: Development during the past twenty years. *Criminal Justice and Behavior, 23,* 162–199.

Marshall, W. L. & Barbaree, H. E. (1990a). An integrated theory of the etiology of sexual offending. In W. L. Marshall, D. R. Laws, & H. E. Barbaree (Eds.), *Handbook of sexual assault: Issues, theories and treatment of the offender.* New York: Plenum Press.

Marshall, W. L. & Barbaree, H. E. (1990b). Outcome of comprehensive cognitive-behavioral treatment programs. In W. L. Marshall, D. R. Laws, & H. E. Barbaree (Eds.), *Handbook of sexual assault: Issues, theories
and treatment of the offender.* New York: Plenum Press.

Note that the listing of multiple-authored papers follows the listing of the single-authored papers,
even though chronologically the multiple-authored chapters were written first.

A judicial opinion in a reference list follows the usual citation format: the names of the parties separated by *v.* and followed by a comma, the volume number of the case reporter, the abbreviation for the case reporter, the first page of the opinion, followed by a comma, and then the year
in parentheses:

Furman v. Georgia, 408 U.S. 238 (1972).

For sources retrieved online, reference citations should include the digital object identifier (DOI)
if this is available. A DOI is a label consisting of numbers and letters that is specific to each
individual source; if a DOI is included in the entry, no additional information about retrieval is
needed. If no DOI is available, citations should include the URL of the home page of the electronic
source. No date of retrieval is needed unless the source is likely to change over time (for example,
a Wikipedia entry), and no page-specific URL is needed unless the source would be extremely
difficult to locate without it. For sources retrieved from an aggregated database (EBSCO,
LexisNexis), do not include the name of the database; instead, include the home page URL for the
journal or periodical you are citing:

Hinton, W. J., Sims, P. L., Adams, M. A., & West, C. (2007). Juvenile justice: A system divided. *Criminal
Justice Policy Review, 18,* 466–475. doi:10.1177/0887403407304578

LaGanga, M. L. (1998, April 10). Death row inmate: Is he now insane? *Los Angeles Times.* Retrieved from
http://articles.latimes.com.

IN-TEXT CITATIONS

It is not enough to simply compose a list of references at the end of the academic paper. It is also
necessary to use in-text citations, or refer the reader to the references you used when citing another author's specific thoughts and ideas. This is done by using the author's last name and the
date of the publication in parentheses. Additionally, if you directly quote the author, then you
also need to include the page number from where you took the quote. The reader can then use
this information to find the full reference on the reference list.

There are two primary ways in which to cite a reference in the text. First, you can put the
author's name and the date of the publication in parentheses at the end of the sentence, like this:

One of the most influential criminological theories today is strain theory (Cao, 2004).

Alternatively, you can mention the author's name in the sentence like this:

According to Cao (2004), strain theory is one of the most influential criminological theories today.

If quoting a statement by Cao, you must include the page number with the citation:

According to Cao (2004, p. 75), "the concept of anomie is elusive and controversial."

Even if you do not quote, but you take several words from the text and paraphrase, you should
cite the page numbers where you read the information. For example:

According to Cao (2004, p. 72), Merton's five modes of adaptation are conformity, innovation, ritualisim,
retreatism, and rebellion.

The reader can then go to the reference list to find out information about the book written by Cao. In the reference list, the reader will see this:

Cao, L. (2004). *Major criminological theories: Concepts and measurement.* Belmont, CA: Wadsworth.

If there are between two and six authors, all are mentioned in the text, like this:

Sexual offenders are considered to be different than other types of offenders (Marshall, Serran, & Marshall, 2006).

The second in-text citation, however, should have the first author's name followed by "et al.," like this: (Marshall et al., 2006). If there are more than six authors, the in-text citation should always just have the first author's name followed by "et al.," such as: (Wolchik et al., 2000).

If a sentence in your text draws upon more than one source, then all are included in the in-text parenthesis, alphabetically, like this:

Many criminological researchers in the last have century have studied strain theory (Agnew, 1992; Cloward & Ohlin, 1960; Cohen, 1955; Messner & Rosenfeld, 1994).

Other Referencing Guidelines

Although the APA format is the one most professors use in criminal justice courses, you should also know about three others also in use: ASA (American Sociological Association), MLA (Modern Language Association), and University of Chicago's *Chicago Manual of Style.* The ASA format is used mostly by professors whose home field is sociology and who are therefore most comfortable with it. The MLA format is used mostly in the humanities, especially literature, and is often the one taught in composition courses involving the research paper. The *Chicago Manual* format is the only one still using footnotes for citation and is decreasing in popularity, although still required by some professors.

All four formats share much in common. In the reference list, all include the same four essential items:

- Author(s)
- Date
- Title
- Publication information

All have the reference list alphabetized by authors' last names and all have each entry done as a hanging indent, as illustrated previously. Each of the four items is followed by a period. All have a citation in the text and then a reference list at the end. ASA and MLA work like APA in that the in-text citation is a parenthesis in a sentence. *Chicago* has a superscript or footnote number in the text and then a footnote at the bottom of the page or an endnote at the end of the chapter or book.

ASA

The ASA format resembles the APA, except that the punctuation conventions differ. In ASA, the comma is omitted in the in-text parenthetical citation:

ASA: Warr 2002 (cf. APA: Warr, 2002).

With two authors, the ampersand (&) in APA is replaced by "and" in ASA:

ASA: Akers and Sellars (cf. APA: Akers & Sellars).

Items on the reference list are the same, except that for ASA the date is not in parentheses and the author's first name is spelled out:

ASA: Warr, Mark. 2002. *Companions in crime: The social aspects of criminal conduct.* Cambridge, England: Cambridge University Press.

cf. APA: Warr, M. (2002). *Companions in crime: The social aspects of criminal conduct.* Cambridge, England: Cambridge University Press.

MLA

MLA used to have a footnote citation system but now resembles APA. MLA has the author's name in parentheses in the text, just as APA does, but omits the date of publication. Because humanities papers, especially in literature, encourage quotation, yet social science papers discourage it, the number in parentheses in MLA format is the page number for quoted or paraphrased material: in MLA, (Warr 25) would mean there's a quote or paraphrase in the text on page 25 of Warr. Most MLA citations in criminal justice papers would just have the author's name (Warr).

The MLA reference list item resembles the ASA's, except that the date of publication is now included with the other publication information:

Warr, Mark. *Companions in crime: The social aspects of criminal conduct.* Cambridge, England: Cambridge University Press, 2002.

CHICAGO

Chicago uses footnotes for citation. There is a superscript or footnote number in the text at an appropriate place, usually the end of the quotation or paraphrase. There is then a footnote with the usual four items at the bottom of the page:

4. Mark Warr, *Companions in Crime: the Social Aspects of Criminal Conduct* (Cambridge, England: Cambridge University Press, 2002), 25.

Notice that the only period in a footnote is at the end. The last number is the page. Subsequent citations to the same source will simply have the author's last name and page number: 6. Warr, 33.

The Reference List item in Chicago is identical in format to that for MLA. One could go into further detail about each of these formats comparable to the discussion of APA offered earlier, but it is hoped that this is sufficient for you to get the idea.

Summary

As is clear from this chapter, college and university libraries can provide a wealth of information in online, book, and journal format for research in the field of criminal justice. Some universities may also subscribe to criminal justice search databases. However, even if your school does not subscribe to criminal justice databases, the list of Internet sources provided in this chapter should offer a place to begin conducting research. Though these sources may appear daunting to the new criminal justice scholar, it is encouraging that so many sources are available in this field and that the search engines can take you as deeply and thoroughly into any subject as you wish or need to go. Knowing about these resources and how to use them is what makes you a professional-in-training. It is important to understand the difference between a popular, nonscholarly website and a scholarly research article on the Internet. Finally, the chapter enables you to make responsible use of the sources you discover.

References

American Psychological Association. (2009). *Publication manual of the American Psychological Association* (6th ed.). Washington, DC: American Psychological Association.

Buzawa, E. S. & Buzawa, C. G. (2002). *Domestic violence: The criminal justice response* (3rd ed.). New York: Sage.

New York State Coalition Against Domestic Violence. (2009). *Domestic violence handbook.* Available at: http://www.nyscadv.org/handbook.htm.

10 | VISUAL **AIDS IN ORAL AND** **WRITTEN** PRESENTATIONS

Students may be required to give oral presentations for a number of reasons, including as part of a classroom assignment, at a conference, or for a criminal justice agency. The presentation may be formal, requiring the student to present statistical information and analyses via PowerPoint, or it may be informal, where the student speaks generally about a criminal justice topic. The key to any presentation is to thoroughly understand the material, know what the audience hopes to achieve by listening to the presentation, and understand the best way to present the material to this particular audience.

METHODS OF ORAL PRESENTATIONS

There are multiple ways in which to give an oral presentation. The most common methods for presenting criminal justice information are: talking without assistance from any written work, writing out the main points of the presentation (on index cards or as bullet points) and using these as talking points throughout the presentation, and creating a PowerPoint presentation. Each of these methods has strengths and weaknesses, and the most suitable method will depend upon the type of presentation, the audience, and the information you need to convey. If you are giving a presentation on criminal justice statistics, for instance, it would be neither beneficial for the audience nor practical for you to talk without assistance from any written work. It is generally not advisable to simply read an entire written paper to the audience, as this will prevent you from making and keeping eye contact, a vital element in keeping audience interest, and the even pace and tone of reading does not allow you to emphasize the key points of the presentation.

There are a number of things to consider in any type of presentation:

- *Length of the presentation.* Usually, a presentation will have a set amount of time. If you are giving an oral presentation as part of a classroom assignment, it is likely that the professor will specify the length of the presentation. Generally, classroom presentations are short. Rarely would a classroom presentation require you to speak for more than fifteen minutes, and the likely length of time would be between five and ten minutes. Otherwise, all students, or student groups, would not have a chance to present their material. If you are presenting information at a conference, the moderator, or chair of the panel, will establish a set amount of time for each presenter. At the American Society of Criminology (ASC) annual conference and the

Academy of Criminal Justice Sciences (ACJS) annual conference, presentations are ten to twenty minutes in length, depending upon the number of presenters per panel.

• **Depth of the presentation.** This is necessarily related to the previous point, as the length of the presentation will dictate the depth of the information you present. Once you know how much time you have to present, you can make a presentation outline. As you would do for a written paper, you should set up the presentation with an introduction, a body, and a conclusion. The depth of the information presented in the introduction and conclusion will likely be the same regardless of the length of the presentation, as you always need to introduce the audience to the topic and summarize the main points for them at the end. It is the body of the presentation that will vary based upon the length of time allotted to you. If you have only five minutes to present, you know you will have time to present only the key issues and the most important supporting details.

• **Time management.** Everyone will present differently, but most people have one thing in common: they are nervous when speaking in front of a group of people. The result of this is that some people speak very quickly, while others speak more slowly than usual or add a lot of unnecessary words to the presentation. It is important that you understand how nervousness affects you so that you can manage your presentation time appropriately. A common problem with presentations is that the presenter takes too much time at the beginning of the talk and is forced to rush through the last part of the talk. Unfortunately, the last part of the presentation is usually the most important, because it is where you tend to present analyses and conclusions. Although you do not want to rush the beginning of the presentation, make sure to spend the most time on the key issues.

• **Handouts.** In some cases, it is beneficial to give the audience a copy of the presentation in the form of a handout. A handout is both something to take away from the presentation and something to consult during it. If your handout is your presentation in essay form, it will be useful in covering everything, but it will also make listening to your presentation unnecessary. It will also be the most trouble and expense to duplicate in great number. You may find it more useful to have a handout of one to three pages keyed to important points in your text, particularly if you are describing charts and statistics. If you give a PowerPoint presentation, you can print handouts of the slides, three or six to a page.

PREPARING FOR A PRESENTATION

When considering how to begin creating an oral presentation, you should first consider what the presentation is for, whether it is also associated with a written paper, how much time you have to present, and whether you are presenting alone or with a co-presenter.

First consider the purpose of the presentation. Is it to convey research results, to summarize the literature on a particular topic, to summarize the main points of a book, or to debate a controversial criminal justice issue? This matters, because it will have an effect on the type of presentation you give. A common oral presentation assignment is to present research findings. Often, professors who require oral presentations also require written research papers on the same topic. Even if a written paper is not required, it is advisable to think of the oral presentation as though you are writing a paper. You will structure the oral presentation in the same format (introduction, body, and conclusion). The introduction includes a few brief statements about the topic and purpose of the presentation. The body includes the main points of the research, the methodology (if applicable), the findings of the research, any research that supports or contradicts these findings, and proposals as a result of the research. The conclusion is a brief summary of the key findings. For this type of presentation, it is useful to use some type of visual aids, handouts, and/or PowerPoint (see following discussion).

Other types of presentations will have formats that vary slightly. For instance, if the purpose of the presentation is to summarize the main points of a book, then the presentation should take the same structure as a book review. The purpose of a book review is to summarize the main points of the book, discuss the positive and the negative aspects of the book, and explain for whom the book would be most appropriate. This presentation will not necessarily follow the format of a research paper, and it is likely to be shorter than the presentation of research results.

Sometimes professors require students to present on group projects. In this case, the co-presenters must determine who will do which part of the presentation. It is advisable to divide the presentation into distinct sections. For instance, take the following assignment in a criminological theory class:

> In groups of three students, choose a theory that best explains organized crime. You will be required to give a 15-minute presentation, which must include:
>
> - An explanation of what organized crime is
> - An explanation of the theory and how it applies to organized crime
> - A policy that would help to combat organized crime, based upon this theoretical explanation

This assignment can easily be segmented into three sections, as noted by the bullets. Because there are three presenters, each presenter should be responsible for a bullet. The professor has not indicated that any segment of this project holds more weight than any other, so students should assume that each part of the project holds equal weight and should be given equal time. It is vital when you do a group project that each member of the group knows what the others are doing to be sure that the three sections work together.

An alternate type of group presentation could be in the form of a debate. Consider the following assignment:

> Groups of two students will choose competing theories to explain a particular crime. Students will have 10 minutes to debate why a particular theory best explains the chosen crime.

In this type of exercise, two students debate a topic. In this assignment, students may choose to explain a burglary through social learning theory and control theory. There are no specific guidelines given, so it is best to prepare for such a debate by thoroughly researching the debate topic, in this case, both burglary and the theory to explain it. Though the debate will take less time than the group presentation (10 minutes compared to 15), the debate requires more work, because the presenters must be prepared to respond to any points made about the crime or the theory. Students should also be prepared to present policy conclusions related to the theory and the crime.

For presentations on book reviews and for debates, it is unlikely that you would need handouts for the audience or other types of visual aids to present information. However, when presenting research results, it is beneficial for the audience to see the material you are presenting. Handouts are one way to convey this information to the audience, and this may be the only way to present information if the classroom or presentation space does not have a computer and a projector. However, if presenting in a technologically "smart" classroom, PowerPoint can be used for the presentation instead.

MICROSOFT POWERPOINT

PowerPoint is a visual tool used for presentations. It is produced by Microsoft as part of Microsoft Office; for more technical information on this product, see http://office.microsoft.com/en-us/default.aspx. It allows for the creation of a series of electronic slides that can be used in a presentation. The purpose of this section of the chapter is not to go step by step through how to use PowerPoint, but rather to explain when it is beneficial to use it and how to use it effectively in a presentation.

Most importantly, it is possible to use PowerPoint only if you have a computer and projector (you could use it simply with a computer screen, but for the purposes of the presentation, a projector is necessary). Many classrooms are now equipped with this technology, particularly at conferences, and PowerPoint lectures and presentations are becoming more common. If your classroom or presentation space does not have this technology, then you must find another method of presenting information. The next question to ask is whether PowerPoint would be useful in conveying information to the audience. Are you presenting statistical findings that may be difficult to understand if they are not seen? Are you presenting visual aids, such as the tables, graphs, and figures discussed shortly? Do you want to include special features, like clip art (pictures or drawings downloaded from the Internet), videos, or audio? Do you want to convey a lot of technical information? If you answered yes to any of these questions, then it would be advisable to use PowerPoint.

The key to a good PowerPoint presentation is brevity; make points succinctly and clearly. PowerPoint should not be used to write out an entire speech. Instead, the slides should contain either visual aids or brief statements, often in bullet format. It is common to begin with a brief overview of the points you plan to cover in the presentation, as follows:

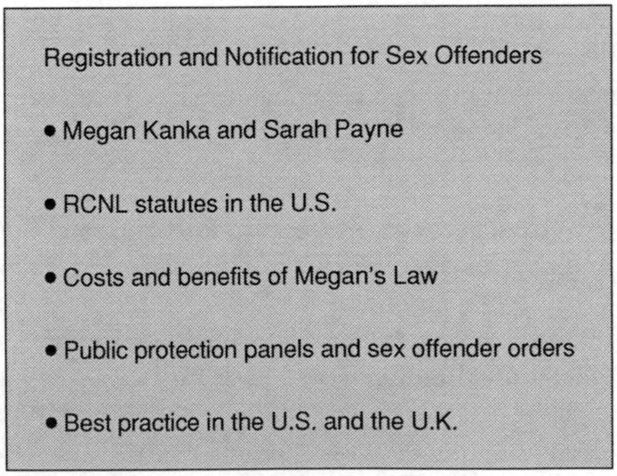

Registration and Notification for Sex Offenders

- Megan Kanka and Sarah Payne

- RCNL statutes in the U.S.

- Costs and benefits of Megan's Law

- Public protection panels and sex offender orders

- Best practice in the U.S. and the U.K.

FIGURE 10.1

Once you begin the presentation, slides should succinctly present information, such as the following, which uses a bullet-point format. This allows the audience to listen to the presentation rather than read too much information.

Issues related to reporting abuse

- Sexual abuse is significantly underreported
- Significant delay in reporting of child sexual abuse
- Factors related to delay in reporting are:
  - age at time of abuse
  - gender of victim
  - relationship to perpetrator
  - acts of abuse committed
  - developmental/cognitive abilities of victim
  - level/type of grooming behavior

FIGURE 10.2

The following PowerPoint slide is a summary slide. Using a table, it concisely discusses four types of child molesters: fixated extra-familial child molesters, fixated intra-familial child molesters, regressed extra-familial child molesters, and regressed intra-familial child molesters. It allows the audience to quickly understand the key issues associated with each typology.

Summary of Child Molester Typologies

	Extra-familial	**Intra-familial**
Fixated offenders	Most serious type of child molester; few or no relationships with agemates; usually diagnosed as a pedophile; many victims likely; high level of recidivism.	Likely to abuse outside the home as well as own children; likely to commit intrusive sexual acts; fewer victims than extra-familial fixated offenders.
Regressed offenders	Prefer sexual relationships with agemates to children; poor socio-sexual skills; rarely continues relationship with the victims for an extended period of time.	Begin offending when experiencing negative affective states or marital problems; children are substitutes for agemates.

FIGURE 10.3

Alternatively, the following is *not* a good PowerPoint slide, because it tries to convey too much information for the audience, despite the use of bullet points. Instead of writing all of these points out, it would have been better to write key words on the PowerPoint slide and communicate the details to the audience verbally. For instance, it would be better to write "Abuse History" for the first bullet on this slide, and explain to the audience that many child molesters have been abused physically and/or sexually.

Characteristics of Child Molesters

- Many were abused physically and/or sexually.
- They have poor social and relationship skills.
- They tend to be socially inept in adult relations.
- They have a low sense of self-esteem.
- They have feelings of inadequacy.
- Many have problems with potency.
- Many have moral inhibitions.
- Some are violent; however, these are rare and tend to be nonincestuous offenders who abuse both girls and boys.
- Most seek a mutually comforting relationship with a child.
- Regressed offenders might revert to adult-child relationships because of a hindrance to normal adult relationships, many have had previously frustrating experiences with adult relations.
- There is a correlation between negative affective states and deviant sexual behaviour for child molesters, mainly inadequacy, stress and loneliness.

FIGURE 10.4

Note that all of the above slides have different backgrounds, fonts, size of type, and formats. It is important when choosing font and size of type to choose what can be read from the rear or side of the room where you are presenting. PowerPoint comes with many template backgrounds for you to choose from, as well as templates for presenting the information (e.g., slides with titles or without, with columns, rows, blank). You can also add logos, such as in the following title slide.

VISUAL AIDS FOR WRITTEN ASSIGNMENTS AND ORAL PRESENTATIONS

A key aim of the research paper or the oral presentation of research is to effectively communicate your points to the audience. Although the majority of the findings will be written, it is also important to convey some of the key findings through the use of various pedagogical tools, particularly tables, figures, and graphs. Once written in a Word or Excel document, these can be placed directly into PowerPoint presentations or passed out as handouts. The information contained in the charts must be clear, concise, and understandable to the audience.

If inserting a visual aid into an article, book, or chapter, you need to follow a particular format. First, it should logically follow the written information directly preceding it. Additionally, the visual aid should be noted in text. For instance, if you are summarizing various theories of crime, at the end of the paragraph before the visual you should point out to the reader that Table X summarizes all the theories of crime discussed in the article. For oral presentations, the same formatting issues apply. It is important to summarize the key points before showing the slide presenting data in chart format.

Examples of visual aids in this chapter will come from a study conducted by one of the authors on child sexual abuse in the Catholic Church (hereafter referred to as "The Bishops'

FIGURE 10.5

Study"). The aim of the study was to explain the nature and scope of child sexual abuse in the Catholic Church in the United States from 1950–2002. It was a descriptive study, the purpose of which was to gather data and help to explain the extent of the crisis and the circumstances surrounding the abuse. It included information on priests with allegations, victims who made allegations, and the church response to the abuse. There were 4,392 priests with allegations and 10,667 victims who made allegations of abuse; because of the large amount of data gathered, it is a good study to use for examples of tables, figures, and graphs.

Tables

Tables are key to presenting data succinctly for the reader. They usually provide summary information for the reader, either in terms of literature or data. Tables come in numerous formats. Though many academic journals will specify the table format they prefer (e.g., grid, list, classic), there is not a preferred table format for presenting criminological data otherwise. Most journals prefer for tables to be simple; in other words, they rarely allow for shading, bold, or italic. In presentations, nearly any type of table is acceptable so long as it is understandable.

In "The Bishops' Study," the author used tables at several points in order to succinctly summarize information for the readers. Table 10.1 is in a simple grid format. It shows the decade that priests with allegations of abuse were ordained. Note that the table has a table number and a title, important information for the reader who looks at the table and doesn't read the text thoroughly.

Table 10.2 is the same table using shading to highlight columns:

And Table 10.3 is the same chart using shading to highlight rows.

You can see that there are many ways to present the same information, depending upon the points you are trying to get across to the audience.

In addition to conveying data, tables can be used to summarize literature. This approach is helpful when writing books or book chapters or agency reports, which tend to be longer and contain a lot of text. You would most likely not use it in an oral report. The table is a way to

Table 10.1 Decade of ordination.

Decade	Count	% of Total
1890–1919	33	0.8%
1920–1929	84	2%
1930–1939	256	6%
1940–1949	523	12.6%
1950–1959	959	23%
1960–1969	1060	25.4%
1970–1979	810	19.4%
1980–1989	344	8%
1990–2000	96	2%
Total	4,167	100%

Table 10.2 Decade of ordination.

Decade	Count	% of Total
1890–1919	33	0.8%
1920–1929	84	2%
1930–1939	256	6%
1940–1949	523	12.6%
1950–1959	959	23%
1960–1969	1060	25.4%
1970–1979	810	19.4%
1980–1989	344	8%
1990–2000	96	2%
Total	4,167	100%

Table 10.3 Decade of ordination.

Decade	Count	% of Total
1890–1919	33	0.8%
1920–1929	84	2%
1930 –1939	256	6%
1940–949	523	12.6%
1950–1959	959	23%
1960–1969	1060	25.4%
1970–1979	810	19.4%
1980–1989	344	8%
1990–2000	96	2%
Total	4,167	100%

Table 10.4		
Author(s), year	**Sample**	**Method**
Andrews, 1999	Four congregations of clergy and parishioners	Self-reports
Flynn, 1999	25 sexually abused women	Self-reports
McDevitt, 1999	Three groups of Roman-Catholic priests to determine the extent of their own personal abuse	Self-reports
Mendola, 1998	277 Catholic priests and religious brothers referred for psychiatric evaluation	Retroactive study examining archival data
Pritt, 1998	115 Mormon women who reported sexual abuse	Questionnaire examining spirituality, concept of God, and optimism and pessimism
Rosetti, 1997	1, 810 Catholics to determine the affect of abuse accusations on their faith in Church and God	Questionnaire
Rosetti, 1995	1,810 Catholics to determine the significance in victim trauma based upon age and gender	Questionnaire
McLaughlin, 1994	Pilot study with adults and children to find out the difference in effects of abuse on their spirituality	Spirituality scale and self-reports
Irons and Laaser, 1994	25 sexually abusive priests who are in treatment	Assessment scales to determine sexual and other addictions
Geotz, 1992	374 ordained pastors to find out how many had affairs	Self-report surveys

break the monotony of text for the reader, summarizing key points of the literature you have just summarized. Table 10.4 is a summary of previous studies on sexual abuse by priests, including their sample and methodology.

Figures

Figures are charts that help to convey a connection between ideas. Although tables are used to list or summarize ideas, figures show how different concepts or stages of a process are linked. Many figures take the shape of flow charts, and this visual tool is useful to the listener or reader in linking ideas discussed in the text. Figure 10.6 shows the "cycle" of societal reaction to child sexual abuse. Note the arrows leading from one text box to the next, clearly indicating the direction of the cycle.

Graphs

Graphs are an excellent way to convey results of a study and are in fact the most visible way to make the audience understand the information. There are many types of graphs. The most

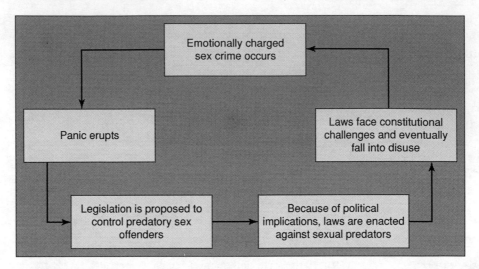

Legislation is proposed to control predatory sex offenders

Because of political implications, laws are enacted against sexual predators

FIGURE 10.6. Cycle of moral panic and reactions to sex offenders *Source:* Terry, K. (2006). *Sexual Offenses and Offenders: Theory Practice and Policy.* Belmont, CA: Wadsworth.

common are the bar graph, line graph, and pie chart, though you will use different graphs depending on the type of statistical analysis you conduct with your data. Graphs can be constructed in many computer applications, most commonly Word, Excel, Access, and PowerPoint. Specialized applications can also be used to create graphs, including SPSS (Statistical Packages for the Social Sciences).

THE BAR CHART

A bar chart is the most common type of chart used to convey information. Bar charts are usually simple and easy to read, and clearly define the variables discussed. It is appropriate to use a bar chart to show a contrast between or within variables.

Much of the data in "The Bishops' Study" consisted of explaining numbers, such as the number of priests with allegations of abuse, the number of victims, the ages of victims, and so on. As such, bar charts were appropriate for much of the material. Figure 10.7 is an example of a bar chart showing the number and age of the victims at the times they were abused by priests.

Bar charts can also be more complex, showing the interaction of two or more variables. Figure 10.8 shows the age and gender of the victims of sexual abuse by priests. Notice that when there are multiple categories represented in the graph, it is necessary to include a legend with the chart explaining the variables. This chart is clear, showing numbers of boys and girls who were abused and the age at which they were abused. Although this information was also included in text form, the visual immediately makes it clear that there were more victims who were male and aged 11–14 years than any other type of victim.

Be careful not to make the bar charts too complex; although it is useful to display information visually to the reader, charts encompassing too much data may be difficult for the reader alone to discern. The following chart is one such example. It refers to the delay in reporting of child sexual abuse events. The point of the chart is to convey that there is a significant delay

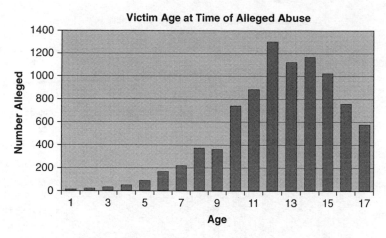

FIGURE 10.7   Example bar chart

FIGURE 10.8   More complex bar chart with legend

between the time that the abuse occurs and when it is reported. Each color of the bars represents a period of delayed time from abuse to reporting. Although this chart may be considered too complex to include in a book or article, it may be a good tool to use in a presentation (when it can be carefully explained by the presenter).

THE PIE CHART

Like the bar chart, the pie chart is an excellent visual tool for the reader. If used correctly, it can provide the reader with a quick understanding of the issue just discussed in the text. Pie charts can contain information in various ways, and the best way to convey information will depend

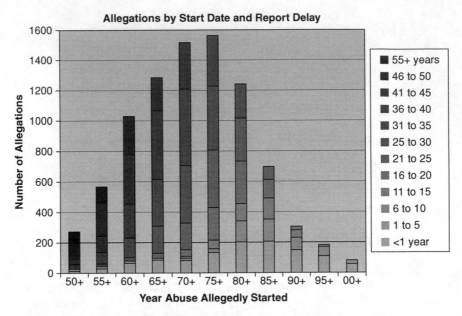

FIGURE 10.9 Data-heavy chart

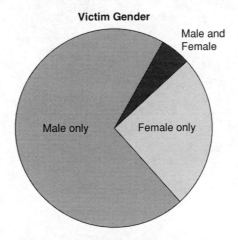

FIGURE 10.10 Example pie chart

upon the number of variables involved and the information that you are trying to convey. The pie chart in Figure 10.10 is a simple chart, describing the gender of the victims of child sexual abuse by Catholic priests. This is visually better than a bar chart because it is clear that the large majority of the victims—more than three-quarters—were male.

Pie charts can be more complex, and can also be labeled differently depending on what you are trying to convey. Figure 10.11 shows the types of enticements that priests gave to their victims in order to make them comply with the abuse. It contains a legend instead of titles within the pie chart. This allows the author to write within the pie chart the percentage of the chart represented by each section of the pie. Also note that only 17 percent of victims received such enticements. In this case,

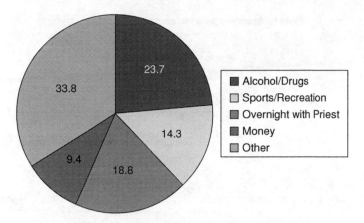

FIGURE 10.11   More complex pie chart: **Types of enticements offered by priests (to 17% of victims)**

the chart shows the percentage of all enticements given. It would also be possible to create a pie chart with one section of the chart showing that 83 percent of the victims were not given enticements. The author chose not to make that type of a chart, because it would condense five sections of information into a small piece of the pie and thus make it difficult to read and interpret.

THE LINE GRAPH

Line graphs are useful if you are aiming to show continuity in several variables, such as showing a phenomenon that occurs over time. Although this can be demonstrated with other charts, such as the bar graph, the bars do not allow for the same level of continuity.

The line graph in Figure 10.12 shows the ordination dates of the priests who had allegations of abuse. The author used a line graph here because the chart discusses ordination dates from 1960–2000, which is a long period of time. A bar graph with 40 bars would not have had the same level of continuity as this line graph. Here, it is clear that 1970 is a peak year of ordination for priests with allegations of child sexual abuse, with 11 percent of priests ordained in that year

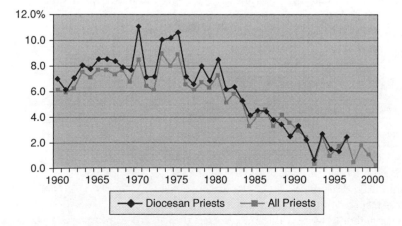

FIGURE 10.12   Example line chart

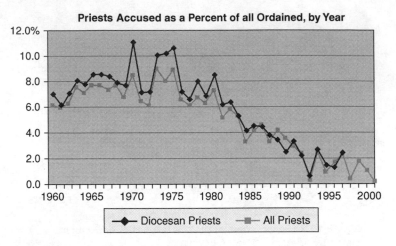

FIGURE 10.13   Line chart in PowerPoint slide

having allegations. If you look back at the section on tables, you will see that the information contained here is also in table format. Which do you think makes the point more clearly?

All of the graphs in these figures can be inserted into a PowerPoint presentation. For instance, the graph in Figure 10.12 in a PowerPoint slide would appear as in Figure 10.13.

Summary

When presenting important points in written work and in oral presentations, it is necessary to present the information clearly and concisely. Visual aids, when used correctly, help to convey this information in a format that the audience can easily comprehend. This is particularly important for oral presentations using PowerPoint or handouts, as oral presentations are usually short and meant to convey a large amount of information quickly. The key to a good presentation, whatever format you use, is to understand the material thoroughly and practice the presentation beforehand. Know how long it will take you to make the presentation, make sure you can succinctly explain the charts, and emphasize the most important points both in the body of the presentation and in a conclusion.

APPENDIX

Grammar and Usage

How to assess the importance of grammatical "correctness" in academic writing is a topic that can be vexing. Though the focus of this book is writing in criminal justice, this "Grammar and Usage Appendix" covers general information about writing that will be useful to all writers.

CORRECTNESS AND APPROPRIATENESS

France has an official body, L'Académie française, to rule on the grammar and diction of the French language. English-speaking countries have no such thing. Bona fide English professors, celebrity journalists, and others write chapters and books telling people what is right, but they do not agree on everything and have no way of enforcing their opinions except to get them widely accepted by people who will then cite them as authorities. Academic grammarians usually engage in descriptive work: they study how people use the language rather than pronounce how they *should* use the language. Dictionaries often walk the line between description and prescription in deciding what words or usages to include and how to label what is included (e.g., "colloquial"), and although it is certainly efficient to settle things by looking them up in "the dictionary" or a grammar manual, these books are built out of thousands of editorial decisions, most but not all of them universally or widely accepted.

Thus, "appropriateness" seems to be a more useful standard than "correctness." What is appropriate is what works in a particular setting. The same item of clothing is appropriate in some settings but not in others. A professor might wear a tuxedo to a wedding but not to teach in, a suit to teach in but not to a pool party. Similarly, try the following exercise. You have forgotten your house key, but fortunately, there is someone home. You ring the bell. "Who is it?" that person asks. What do you answer? "It's me." But what if a professor told you that "It's me" is grammatically incorrect? The construction calls for the nominative case: "It is I." Would you switch, even though "It's me" may sound more appropriate for the informal situation? Though correct, "It is I" seems less appropriate in such a situation.

There is nothing strange or controversial about varying language in different social contexts, and people do it all the time. People talk in slang or colloquialisms, use sentence fragments, use incorrect grammar, and borrow words from other languages. These are fine for informal discussions or written communications (e.g., through email or instant messaging), but not in a formal speech or for an academic paper. It is efficient to talk in sentence fragments, as in, "Where are you going?" "To the movies," not "I am going to the movies." However, academic writing requires a higher level of formality. It is important to understand how and when errors occur so as to fix such errors in formal writing.

Error and Intelligibility

Anyone who has studied for national or university-wide writing exams, like the ACT or anything administered by the ACT company, may know that these days such exams foster a particular view of error. For one thing, most of these exams are graded holistically, which means that the scorer's recognition of writing errors is part of an overall impression that includes organization, development, sophistication of diction, and other things. Strength in other areas will outweigh a small amount of error. ACT distinguishes between "local" and "global" error. A "local" error happens once or twice and does not interfere with understanding. "Global" errors form a pattern in the writing and make the writing hard to comprehend. Local errors may be overlooked in the scoring, largely as a result of many students who speak English as a foreign language. The purpose of the writing is to express thoughts and convey information, and local errors still allow this to occur.

On the other hand, academic professors may not adopt such criteria when they are grading student course work. Grading is not a holistic exercise. Feedback may trigger improvement. Tolerance varies. Some teachers of content courses may not want to deal with perceived error at all and may grade entirely on content. Others may stress their functions as gatekeepers to a profession and be quite unforgiving even of perceived errors that do not impede understanding. It is critically important to read through academic writing multiple times prior to submitting it for a grade. This will reduce the local errors and likely improve the expression of the content as well.

One of the authors of this text, beginning to teach a course called "Legal Writing," was told the following story by a lawyer colleague:

> A will is being probated. It says, "I wish the remainder of my estate to be divided between Mr. A, Miss B, Mrs. C, and Mr. D." The lawyer for Mr. A tells the judge, "My client gets half and the others share the other half. *Between* means 'by twain' and is used with two. If the deceased meant the four to share equally, the will would have used *among*." Do you think the deceased really meant Mr. A to get half? The law requires precise use of language, and lawyers are trained to take advantage of ambiguities in language. Lawyers who do not get it right are vulnerable.

What Does This All Mean?

All students entering college need to become deliberate and knowledgeable about the way they use language. This book focuses on the types of assignments and methods of writing in criminal justice, but it is important to be aware of general use of language as well. This is particularly important because the increase in informal communications (e.g., texting) means that writing in proper, formal English requires substantial motivation to learn what is correct and practice it in all classes.

The remainder of this appendix addresses common writing problems. To improve writing requires two things: knowing what the problem is and being willing to fix it. Most students will have specific difficulties with writing (e.g., a misunderstanding of when to use a semicolon). It is important to recognize these problems and practice fixing them. Much language use is habitual, and sometimes writing good academic prose is just a matter of losing bad habits and picking up good ones. This list of problems is not exhaustive by any means; there are many more grammatical errors than are listed here. However, this is an overview of common problems with students who are new to writing at the college level. If you need clarification or more knowledge or more practice, there are more extensive books on grammar (see Strunk & White's *Elements of Style*) that can assist you.

Finally, a point about timing. It is generally best to worry about errors in the last stage of the writing process. Worrying about errors gets in the way of composing, of generating content. Save grammatical proofreading and editing until you have completed a draft of the paper. You can also use spellcheckers and grammar checkers while writing, but it is important to understand their limitations. Spellcheckers have word lists and will flag any word not on the list, so most people's names or technical terms will come up as misspellings. They do not read for content, so they won't catch it if you write *to* instead of *too*. Grammar checkers are even less trustworthy. They get easy subject–verb agreement situations right but miss the hard ones for the same reasons you do, such as when they misidentify the subject. Thus, although these are helpful, you should not rely solely on them.

SENTENCE STRUCTURE

Fragments

Academic English is written in complete sentences. A group of words nominated for a sentence, beginning with a capital letter and ending with a period or question mark (almost never an exclamation mark in academic writing), should be a grammatical sentence. When it isn't, we call it a *fragment*.

"Sentence" is hard to define, but to simplify it has two aspects, both required. In meaning, it expresses a complete thought. In structure, it has a subject and predicate, where the subject is not preceded by a subordinating conjunction like *when* or *if*. By a complete thought, we mean that the sentence needs no other information from some other sentence to stand alone, to make sense. By contrast, consider conversation, which often is carried on in fragments:

"Where did the cops take Charlie?"

"The thirteenth precinct."

"The thirteenth precinct" is a sentence fragment, lacking both subject and verb, but it causes no problem in the context of the conversation. We do not need "The cops took Charlie to," even though that addition would keep the sentence from being a fragment, because it is an answer to a question that provides the missing information. The fragment is missing a subject, the noun *cops* to indicate the doer of the action, and a predicate, a verb indicating the action, such as *took*, but these are provided by context. Fragments are efficient in conversation because they save time and, if misunderstood, the listener can always request clarification, which in practice is inevitably a complete sentence.

Nouns name. The subject of a sentence is the noun or pronoun (a word that substitutes for a noun, like *she*) that names what the sentence is about. A simple subject is the single word noun or pronoun. There are often complex subjects where other words accompany the noun, such as determiners (*the, some, two*) or adjectives (*angry*). "Two angry cops" contains the simple subject "cops" in the complex subject "two angry cops." Verbs convey actions or states of being and are the basis of sentence predicates. Predicates usually include additional words, such as the direct object "Charlie" and the prepositional phrase, "to the thirteenth precinct" which go along with the verb "took" in our example:

Two angry cops took Charlie to the thirteenth precinct.

Grammatically, the inclusion of a subject and verb make something a *clause*. A group of words lacking either or both is a *phrase*. A mere phrase nominated for a sentence will be a sentence fragment. But there are two kinds of clauses, independent and dependent. Independent clauses become dependent if they are preceded by a subordinating conjunction, a word like *because*. A subordinating conjunction keeps the clause from being independent, and therefore a potential sentence, because it suggests missing information. "Because two angry cops took Charlie to the thirteenth precinct" makes us look for information about what happened next. If you read it aloud, your ear does not provide the kind of pause that signals a period but rather the kind of pause that anticipates something else. A third kind of clause, a relative clause, has a relative pronoun (*who, which, that*) as its subject: it is like a subordinate clause in that it also cannot stand alone and needs information from the rest of the sentence to clarify the antecedent of the relative pronoun. Relative clauses also fail the ear test; they're not questions and something is obviously missing before, and perhaps after, the relative clause.

The trick to correcting fragments is to spot them. Nearly everyone can spot fragments in grammar book exercises, because they are presented in a context of looking for fragments and are easy to isolate. Spotting your own fragments is much harder:

- Nearly all fragments are separated parts of the preceding sentence, where the student has put a period and a capital letter where either a comma or no punctuation is called for.
- Nearly all fragments are just providing more information, with a desired pause for emphasis, about a noun or verb in the preceding sentence; they are either adjectival or adverbial in modifying that noun or verb.
- Because nearly all fragments are just extensions of the sentence before them, they are hard to catch; the reader just mentally attaches them and ignores the sentence boundary created by the period.

Here is a typical fragment in an essay: *"The jury should always have the presumption of innocence. Even though they know the trial is the result of a police investigation and deliberation by the district attorney."[1] The second part is an afterthought to the first, modifying the sense of "presumption of innocence."

The way to spot fragments, first of all, is to look for them. The way to look for them is to read your essay backward, beginning with the last sentence, then the one before it, and so on. Because nearly all fragments are parts of the sentence before them, you will come upon the fragment before the preceding sentence. Then you'll spot it.

Once spotted, fragments are easy to fix. Usually, just get rid of the period and capital letter and attach them to the previous sentence. If you prefer, add what is missing, the subject or verb or both:

> The jury should always have the presumption of innocence, even though they know the trial is the result of a police investigation and deliberation by the district attorney.

> The jury should always have the presumption of innocence. They should do this even though they know the trial is the result of a police investigation and deliberation by the district attorney.

Run-on Sentences

Remember that an independent clause has a subject and verb with no subordinating conjunction like *although* preceding the subject. A nominated sentence that does not have an independent clause is a *fragment*. One that has more than one independent clause without proper punctuation is a *run-on*. There are two kinds of run-ons: a *fused sentence* has no punctuation between the independent clauses, and a *comma splice* has only a comma. Both are sources of confusion and there's not much difference between them, although the comma splice is a bit more sophisticated and is favored by some fiction writers. What matters is the inclusion of two or more independent clauses; the inclusion of dependent clauses or modifying phrases does not affect the outcome.

---

[1]An asterisk (*) before an example indicates that it is nonstandard.

Here is a fused sentence:

*Although the Minneapolis experiment looked persuasive, arresting the abusive spouse doesn't always help the situation some angry spouses take the arrest out on their mates.

Here is the same thing as a comma splice:

*Although the Minneapolis experiment looked persuasive, arresting the abusive spouse doesn't always help the situation, some angry spouses take the arrest out on their mates.

A run-on usually comes about when a writer wants to put two independent clauses closely together and therefore doesn't want to put them into separate sentences. That usually happens when the second clause is an explanation or a qualification of the first. Unfortunately, the writer may not know about or be afraid of the semicolon. Unlike the comma, which is oft-used but presents difficulties, the semicolon is seldom used but quite easy. The semicolon's main, and just about only, job is to separate two independent clauses:

Although the Minneapolis experiment looked persuasive, arresting the abusive spouse doesn't always help the situation; some angry spouses take the arrest out on their mates.

Though the semicolon is normally the easiest and most effective way to fix a run-on, it is by no means the only way. One could make a separate sentence out of each independent clause by using a period followed by a capital letter. This is a grammatical solution, but it gives up on what the writer initially wanted to do, that is, to yoke the two clauses together without the full stop of a period. A solution to the comma splice is to add a coordinating conjunction (*and, but, or, nor, for, yet, so*) after the comma, but unless the conjunction is useful, it is a wasted and perhaps confusing addition. Finally, another solution is to turn one of the two independent clauses into a dependent clause by adding a subordinating conjunction before the subject:

Although the Minneapolis experiment looked persuasive, arresting the abusive spouse doesn't always help the situation, because some angry spouses take the arrest out on their mates.

As in the solution involving a coordinating conjunction, the subordinating conjunction helps only if it's useful. Besides having to think up the right one, you might not want to deemphasize the information by subordinating the clause.

A final warning: the use of conjunctive adverbs like *however, consequently*, and *nonetheless* makes no difference in this situation. Although *however* and *but* look like they do the same job, the first is a conjunctive adverb, not a subordinating conjunction; it is part of the clause after it rather than conjoining the two clauses. That's why *however* in such a circumstance is preceded by a semicolon; it is the semicolon rather than the *however* that is doing the job.

Though proofreading for run-ons may look like proofreading for fragments, it is more like checking for subject–verb agreement. One spots independent clauses by looking for subject–verb combinations that lack preceding subordinating conjunctions.

Dangling Modifiers

A modifier is a phrase with a past or present participle that modifies, or provides information about, the subject of the main clause: "Jogging in the park, she was accosted by two men." The modifier is built on the present participle *jogging* and provides information about the subject of the main clause, *she*. Modifiers are said to dangle when there is no appropriate subject to the main clause to attach the modifier to: *"Jogging in the park, two men accosted her," where it is not the two men who are jogging.

An example with a past participle would be: "Stolen, the jewelry needed to be fenced." If it said, *"Stolen, he needed to fence the jewelry," it would imply that "he" was stolen. Such errors are the result of hasty composition and are easily caught and fixed if noticed. Occasionally, dangling modifiers result in unintended humor and damage writer/reader relations. Most errors make writers look careless; dangling modifiers make them look clownish.

SUBJECT–VERB AGREEMENT

Subjects agree with verbs for both number (singular, plural) and person (first, second, third). Because except for the highly irregular *to be* the past tense doesn't alter from one person to the next, it is only in the third person present tense that the problem comes up. Singular nouns; the pronouns *he, she,* or *it*; and the singular indefinite pronouns (*anybody, anyone, each, either, everybody, everyone, everything, neither, no one, one, someone,* or *something*) take -s or -es on the verb: "A thief steals." When the subject and verb are as simple as that and right next to each other, few have problems. The chief exception is those who speak a dialect that omits the -s in the third person as some dialects do because the -s is essentially providing redundant information. Speakers of such dialects need merely to recognize that here is a difference between the way they speak to friends and family and the way they do academic writing and adjust accordingly.

Most people don't leave the -s off most of the time. If you have a subject–verb agreement problem, you need to inspect your writing to see where it comes up and then be on the alert when you proofread for those situations. Difficulties usually arise when more than one noun appears before the verb or when the subject and verb are separated by other words. Then you may have trouble recognizing which noun is the subject:

- The object of a preposition cannot be the subject of a sentence: "The head of the Department of Corrections is a woman." Only "head" can be the subject; both "Department" and "Corrections" are preceded by "of." "Corrections" may be the noun closest to the verb but it is not the subject.
- "There" is not the subject of a sentence beginning with "there." It is just a place marker: the actual subject follows the verb: "There are truants standing on that streetcorner."
- When a relative pronoun (*who, which, that*) is the subject of the verb, the verb agrees with whatever singular or plural noun the relative pronoun is standing in for.
- Two or more singular subjects linked by *and* take a plural verb: "John Wilkes Booth and Lee Harvey Oswald are presidential assassins."
- Two or more singular subjects linked by *either/or* take a singular verb: "Either Sam or Harold is the thief."

Grammar checkers tend to get only the easiest of these correct, so you must be alert to the sorts of situations when you may leave the -s out and proofread for them.

Some subject–verb agreement errors are caused not so much by ignorance of subject–verb agreement as by misunderstanding whether the subject is singular or plural. Some words ending in -s are singular, such as mathematics and criminalistics. A title is singular even if it has a plural in it, for example, the once-famous ad for a Hitchcock movie: "*The Birds* is coming." Although "count" nouns can be either singular or plural ("Two dollars are on the table"), "noncount" nouns are always singular ("Money is on the table").

PRONOUNS

Pronouns tend to present problems in two ways: pronoun–antecedent agreement and case. Pronoun–antecedent agreement is similar to subject–verb agreement in that students who do not know whether a noun takes a singular or plural verb won't know whether it takes a singular or plural pronoun. Pronoun–antecedent agreement means a pronoun (*he, she, it, they*) has to agree in number and gender with the noun it substitutes for, called its antecedent because we always have a noun before we can substitute a pronoun for it. As in the trickier subject–verb agreement situations, pronouns are separated from their antecedents by other words, even other nouns, and proofreaders need to make sure the pronoun is aligned with the right noun. For instance:

Forensic scientists in real life take longer than *they* do on TV to reach *their* conclusions.

As with subject–verb agreement, objects of prepositions are not subjects of sentences ("in . . . life"). A good clue to the number of the pronoun is the number of the verb. Because *take* is plural, the pronoun would be plural too.

Sometimes students who are trying to avoid sexist language have picked up the trick of using "she" or "her" as an all-purpose pronoun, on the grounds that people who object to "he" or "him" as sexist won't object to the feminine: "The detective shouldered her gun." The problem is when it becomes so thoughtless as to refer to men: *"As DA, Rudy Giuliani was noted for her aggressiveness."

Unlike nouns, pronouns, except for *you*, change form to indicate *case*, whether subject or object, and must have the proper case form depending on their use in the sentence: "He sold the drugs to him." This is not usually a source of difficulty, but the exceptions come in compounds where the first item has no case indicator, either because it is a noun or because it is *you*: *"Between you and I, the courts are too lenient," where the preposition *between* takes the object *me*, or *"The suspect and *her* were in the hotel room all night," where *she* is the subject of the verb.

The confusion of *who/whom* is like any other confusion of pronoun case. You might find it helpful to think of *whom* as like *him* or *them*. In all three situations, the objective case is indicated by -m. A good test for when to use *whom, him,* or *them* is if the following word is a verb. If it's a verb, the pronoun before it is likely to be its subject: *he, she, it, they, who*. Similarly, if the word before the pronoun is a preposition like *to* or *for*, the pronoun will be the object of the preposition: *him, her, it, them, whom*.

VERB FORMS

Except for *be*, the most used and therefore the least regularized of the verbs, other verbs have five forms:

- Basic: *detect, steal*
- Present tense third-person singular: *detects, steals*
- Past tense: *detected, stole*
- Past participle: *detected, stolen*
- Present participle: *detecting, stealing*

In these examples, the first verb is regular in that it just adds endings (-s, -ed, -ing); the second is irregular in that it changes spelling. One source of error is assuming that all verbs are regular (*goed). Another is confusing one form of an irregular verb for another, particularly using the past tense as past participle (*"he has stole"). The participles, both past and present, use helping verbs and do not stand alone: "He has stolen the book." "He is stealing the book." "The book was stolen."

Newly coined verbs are always regular: "The detective eyeballed the crime scene," and so on. Unfortunately, many of the most commonly used verbs are irregular; in fact, they stay irregular because they are so old and so common that everyone uses them and most people know how to use them. Although there are commonalities and regularities among irregular verbs (the -en ending for past participles reminds us of the language's Germanic ancestry), it probably makes more sense just to memorize verb forms than to try to memorize rules.

Tenses: Simple, Perfect, Progressive

There are six tenses in English, three simple (past, present, future) and three perfect (present perfect, past perfect, and future perfect). We mostly write in the simple present or past tense, occasionally in the future, but not usually for very long. The perfect tenses depend on past, present, or future constructions of the helping verb *have* and are used to indicate actions or events occurring before what is in the simple past, present, or future. "Violent crime statistics have been down for years, but this year they are up" (a present perfect before a simple present). "The condemned man will have waited years in a cell before he will be executed" (future perfect before future). Any of these tenses can be made progressive, describing something in progress, by using the -ing participle: "The prisoner may have been waiting for years before the appeal is heard."

Confusion comes from using the wrong tense to indicate meaning. It also comes from meaningless *shifts* in tense, from past to present to back without anything happening in the content to justify the shift. *"The officer ran down the block. She sees what looks like a gun in the suspect's hand. She told him to drop the gun and put up his hands." Start with a tense, usually the past, and stay in it.

DICTION AND SPELLING

Diction problems involve use of words that don't exist or words that don't mean what you think they do. They can be seriously confusing. Spellcheckers may catch the first sort if the word invented is not in their dictionary; they probably won't catch the second. A possible remedy for diction errors is to try to avoid being pretentious and make do with words you are sure of. John Dillinger is a hero to English professors, because with a limited vocabulary and a Tommy gun, he managed to rise to the top of his profession. Still, learning any discipline, including criminal justice, is partly a matter of learning new words, and mastering the content often involves mastering the vocabulary. You should not be afraid to use important new words that convey useful meanings, like *jurisdiction* or *recidivism*. It's just that if you are told you got them wrong, you must recognize the problem and work to get them right.

A solution for diction problems is probably the same as a solution for spelling problems. You don't have to know the meaning of every word, just the ones you want to use and have trouble with. Similarly, you don't have to know how to spell every word, just the ones you want to use which you misspell. The solution is to buy a cheap address book and use it to make your own private diction and spelling error dictionary. Every time you are told you misspelled or misunderstood a word, write it down under the appropriate letter in your blank address book cum dictionary. Indicate correct spelling for misspelled words and correct meaning for misunderstood words. If you go to write down a word and find that it is already in your error dictionary, it is a particularly troubling word for you and needs special diligence. Becoming aware of your own spelling and vocabulary demons is the first step to eliminating them.

JARGON

Jargon is the vocabulary of the discipline that has meaning for those in the discipline but not for those outside it. When the vocabulary is the usual method of conveying meaning in the discipline, using it is efficient and also signals your acquisition of disciplinary expertise. Police learn how to talk on police radios. Lawyers learn the words to frame objections in the courtroom. But police may not be understood by citizens if they talk to them the way they talk to other police, and lawyers do not assume that the jury understands the words they aim at the judge and other lawyers. Jargon is specialized diction that is judged by its appropriateness to the purpose and audience of the statement or writing. It should not be used to lay people unless accompanied by necessary explanation, and it would usually be better to try translating the term into everyday vocabulary. Those in the discipline want and are served by the jargon; those outside do not want it and are badly served by it.

That being said, every discipline has some jargon that serves no useful purpose or a purpose that, perhaps useful, is also dubious. Some lawyers love Latin phrases, like *inter alia*, that convey no unique legal meaning but just make the lawyer sound learned. Such jargon should be pruned.

PUNCTUATION

The Apostrophe

The apostrophe (') may be a dying punctuation mark, judging from how much confusion there seems to be about it and how often one sees it misused in print. Its proper use these days is seen as a sign of education and care in writing, so anyone wishing to make a good impression will work at getting it right. We need to look at how to use it and how *not* to use it.

Apostrophes are used in *contractions* and *possessives*. Contractions join two words by omitting one or more letters and substituting an apostrophe for the missing letter(s). Such contractions are I'll (I will), let's (let us), it's (it is), and don't (do not). Besides leaving the apostrophe out, students sometimes think it indicates word separation, when in fact it indicates a missing letter. Contractions are somewhat informal, and it might not be a bad idea if you avoided the problem by not using contractions in academic writing, such as using "cannot" for "can't."

The apostrophe in *possessives* is more troubling. A possessive is used when the noun or pronoun has or possesses the noun or noun phrase following it: "the criminal's intent," "his murder." Apostrophes are involved in the possessive of singular and plural nouns but not in the possessives of pronouns. *His* and *its* may end in -s, but other possessive pronouns do not (*your, her, their*), and none of them takes an apostrophe. "It's" is the contraction of "it is," not the possessive. Singular possessive nouns end in -'s; plural possessive nouns merely have an apostrophe after the plural ending -s, as in "criminals' intentions." Irregular plurals that do not end in -s add -'s, as in "men's." Proper nouns that end in -s may add either just the apostrophe or -'s, depending on the style manual or dictionary in use: "Keats' letters," "Charles' motives," "James's boat."

A good test of whether a noun should be possessive, and therefore end with an apostrophe or -'s, is whether it is followed by a noun. One cannot have two nouns together unless the first possesses the second: "John's gun," not *"John gun."

Complicated as that is, it would be nice if one could stop there. Alas, the real problem with apostrophes is not where they're left out but where they're dropped. One too often sees apostrophes used for simple plurals, as if anytime one adds an -s one adds an apostrophe. Doing that makes an awfully bad impression.

Dashes and Exclamation Points

Both of these punctuation marks are signs of informal writing and should be avoided, or at least minimized, in academic writing. Dashes tend to work as informal colons, indicating that what follows is an explanation or addition. Sometimes dashes just function to loosen sentence structure. You want to avoid making your writing look like jotting when you have, in fact, been careful to compose it. Exclamation points inject emotion into writing. You want your writing to look reasonable, not emotional. If it has an emotional impact, it should come from the content and be earned, not goosed by punctuation.

Commas

Students are often scared of the easy-to-use semicolon but fearless with the rather difficult comma. Semicolons are rare because they just separate closely related independent clauses, but commas have several uses and complexities inside these uses.

COMMA USE 1: SETTING OFF NONRESTRICTIVE ADJECTIVE CLAUSES. An adjective modifies, or provides information about, a noun. An adjective clause begins with who, which, or that and modifies or provides information about the subject or object of the sentence. A restrictive adjective clause provides information necessary to identify the noun, and because it is necessary, it is not set off by commas: "The policeman who is in the room witnessed the beating." The subject is not any policeman but the policeman in the room. "Who is in the room" is restrictive, necessary to identify the subject. On the other hand, "Officer Jones, who was impatient to see his girlfriend, rushed through his testimony." Here we know who Officer Jones is but get information about him. The clause is nonrestrictive and cut off by commas.

"He shot at the policeman who was guarding the exit." There is no comma, because we need the *who* clause to identify the policeman shot at. "He shot at the policeman, who was seriously wounded." We know who was shot and get additional information about his condition.

A test for nonrestrictive clauses is to try omitting the material between the commas. If the sentence still makes sense, you need the commas.

COMMA USE 2: SETTING OFF APPOSITIVES. This is really like the first use, except that instead of a clause, there is a noun phrase. "Harry Doaks, a history professor at the university, is a convicted felon." What's inside the commas is additional information about Doaks, not necessary for his identification. "My uncle Harry is a convicted felon." Unless you know that I have only one uncle, we need his name to identify him. The same test works for appositives as for nonrestrictive adjective clauses; if it can be left out without damaging the clarity of the sentence, it is providing additional information and is cut off by commas.

COMMA USE 3: SEPARATING COORDINATE ADJECTIVES. When two or more adjectives are bunched up in front of a noun, they may be separated by commas. This happens only when they are coordinate, when we can reverse their order, or when we can separate them with and. Most adjectives are coordinate, but not adjectives of age, color, nationality, and material. For these there is an inflexible left-to-right order: "a new blue American cotton shirt." Compare a "wrinkled, greasy shirt," which could just as well be a "greasy, wrinkled shirt."

COMMA USE 4: SEPARATING ITEMS IN A SERIES. A series consists of three or more nouns, verbs, adjectives, adverbs, phrases, or clauses. We put a comma after each item in the series (sometimes except for the last item, depending on your style manual's recommendation) and, usually, put an "and" before the last item. When the items are short—that is, single words—many people leave out the comma before the "and," though it is always right to include it and some say it is always necessary to avoid confusion. Still, "Smith proved to be a thief, liar and murderer," is not confusing.

Though a series of independent clauses would override the rule against comma splices, separating each independent clause with a comma until the ", and" before the last, this grammatically correct ploy is probably unadvisable unless the independent clauses are fairly short and simple. The difficulty in reading that comma splices cause, the confusion about where the clause ends, would still persist even in the grammatically correct series. In that case, many people use semicolons for a complex series of clauses, even though commas are grammatically sufficient.

COMMA USE 5: SEPARATING INDEPENDENT CLAUSES WITH A COORDINATING CONJUNCTION. What if you only have two independent clauses, not a series? If you have the "and" before the second independent clause, you do not need a semicolon and may use a comma instead. In fact, if the clauses are short and simple, many people would just have the "and" and omit the comma: "Jimmy Walker was beloved as a mayor and he was a scoundrel." This rule works with any of the coordinating conjunctions: but, or, not, for, yet, and so, as well as, but we tend not to omit commas before the others.

COMMA USE 6: SEPARATING INTRODUCTORY DEPENDENT CLAUSES AND INTRODUCTORY PHRASES. Normally, in a sentence, the independent clause comes first. When it doesn't, when it is preceded by something else, the something else gets separated from the independent clause by a comma. This works for dependent clauses beginning with a subordinating conjunction: "When Christmas comes, more people think of suicide." It works for prepositional phrases: "At dusk, the crime rate goes up." It works for introductory interjections: "Truly, people behave better in small towns."

OTHER COMMA USES. The comma is a very handy punctuation mark and we cannot list every use it has. It separates items in dates (July 11, 1940), in places (Brooklyn, New York) and in multiple-digit numbers (12,313). It separates such introductions as "he says" or "she wrote" from the quotations they introduce. These are conventions, and most people do not have trouble with them

REFERENCES

Strunk, W. & White, E. B. (1979). *The Elements of Style* (3rd ed.). Boston: Allyn & Bacon.

INDEX